Praise for **Disruptors, Discounters, and Doubters**

[T]he suggestions are really good. They're the kinds of things that conscientious agents would implement, which means that conscientious brokers would support those efforts. And even if it's only 20% of the agents who implement his suggestions, that's 20% better than today, so it's an improvement. I recommend the book!

-Rob Hahn, Notorious R.O.B

Joe Rand is a smart, strategic, and knowledgable straight shooter about real estate. He identifies trends, interprets events, and finds ways broker owners an agents can adapt to rapidly changing circumstances. He pulls no punches, and captures a deep understanding of the real estate industry and where it must go to survive.

-Brad Inman, Inman News

Disruptors, Discounters, and Doubters

Disruptors, Discounters, and Doubters

A Guide for the Client-Oriented Future of the Real Estate Industry

Joe Rand

ISBN 978-1-947635-04-3 (Paperback Edition)
ISBN 978-1-947635-05-0 (Ebook Edition)

Printed in the United States of America
First Printing January 2018
Published by Hart Place Publishing
hartplacebooks.com
info@hartplacebooks.com

Contents

Foreword

JOE RAND IS A SMART, STRATEGIC, AND KNOWLEDGEABLE straight shooter about real estate. He identifies trends, interprets events, and finds ways broker owners and agents can adapt to rapidly changing circumstances.

He was raised in a real estate family and has been a lawyer, a brokerage operator, and a keen observer and writer about the business. Because he's dialed into the industry—its nuances and its leaders— Rand is an expert speaker and savvy moderator at industry events.

He is a regular contributor to my own Inman News and a highly popular speaker at our events, drawing big crowds and lots of readers. Why? Because when he talks, the industry listens.

This book, *Disruptors, Discounters, and Doubters*, captures his deep understanding of the industry and where it must go to survive. Here, he identifies five key changes that the industry must face to serve a new generation of clients.

He challenges those of us in the industry to stop being cookie-cutter salespeople. He insists the industry does a terrible job demonstrating its value to a more discerning and demanding public. And he concludes that the industry is internally in a state of crisis mentally.

Rand pulls no punches, and I assure readers they will come away with a new vision and renewed resolve to better their services and their outlook for the future.

Throughout the book, Rand looks not just at problems, but offers pragmatic solutions for better serving consumers, improving the sales and transaction process, and boosting industry morale.

On a more practical level, Rand writes about improving the process of buying and selling homes through innovative technology and by making the steps of owning a home more streamlined and consumer friendly. He calls for making the process faster, cheaper, and easier. Who can argue with that?

"It's not about us anymore," he says. And I agree.

This book is packed with stories and examples and is a serious but fun and useful read that will help improve the industry. And that fits perfectly with the Joe Rand vibe and legacy because he is a passionate change agent.

Brad Inman, Founder of Inman, real estate's leading name in news, information, and innovation

Preface

"I HAD THIS IDEA FOR MY START-UP when I had a terrible experience with the real estate industry."

One after another, they all said the same thing. A series of young entrepreneurs, almost all of whom had bought or sold a home and were surprised at the horror of the typical real estate transaction.

And they were all trying to change the real estate industry. From the outside.

I watched this all as a judge at the inaugural Realogy FWD Innovation Summit five years ago, where fifteen technology start-ups competed for a $25,000 prize in front of some of the top real estate minds in the industry. It was a fun event that has since become a yearly tradition in the industry and the first place I found out about innovative companies such as Matterport, Updater, and RealScout.

As a real estate broker, though, it was disturbing to see how so many of these start-ups were birthed by frustration with the real estate experience. For example, tech entrepreneur Jonathan Aizen told the story of buying a house in the San Francisco Bay Area with his wife. Interestingly, he had nothing bad to say about his agent. In fact, he said he'd hire that agent again. But he still found the process of buying a home incredibly complicated and exasperating—too much time, too many documents, too many steps, and not enough guidance through the process. So he created a company now called Amitree, which provides both agents and clients with customized checklists that guide them through the process of managing their transactions. He's working to create a better real estate transaction.

But not every tech start-up is inclined to help the real estate industry provide a better experience for our clients. Indeed, FWD was the brainchild of the former Realogy CEO and President Alex

Perriello, who created the competition because he was kept awake at night that "some kid in his garage" would create a way to solve the vexing transactional process without anyone in the industry even knowing about it.

Essentially, Perriello was concerned about what's called "disruption"—the idea of a groundbreaking innovation that either creates a completely new market or provides such an improvement over prevailing technologies that it displaces an existing industry. For example, when was the last time you bought, or even looked at, an encyclopedia? That whole industry was disrupted by the internet, particularly sites such as Wikipedia, and ultimately destroyed. Same goes for the white pages, calculators, and camera film—those industries all got disrupted by technological change and, in many cases, rendered extinct.

Could the same thing happen to the real estate industry? It's possible. We all saw what happened to travel agents when then-start-ups like Expedia and Travelocity invaded their space. And certainly all you need to do is attend Brad Inman's twice-yearly Real Estate Connect conference to see a procession of new kids on the block, many of them start-ups seeking to connect buyers and sellers directly without the need for so-called middleman real estate agents and brokers.

And it's not just about these wannabe Disruptors. We also face a more banal challenge from what we'll call the Discounters—companies that try to replicate the services provided by traditional brokers and agents, but at a fraction of the expense. You'll see them at FWD and Connect as well, and these are firms whose only innovation is that they provide a stripped-down service to clients in exchange for a stripped-down fee.

Some provide basic marketing services, like photos, floor plans, and syndication on their own site and to real estate portals. Others also join the local MLS and offer their listings out for a nominal cooperating broker commission, so they can say that they're providing the same service as traditional brokers and agents.

We've been facing Discounters like this for eons, but they've now become rampant as internet technology has leveled part of the playing field, allowing just about anyone to do basic marketing and online listing distribution.

Overall, though, the biggest challenge the real estate industry faces is from within, from the Doubters—the self-hating agents and brokers who don't believe in the value that the industry provides. They panic every time they see an article in the *New York Times* about some "revolutionary" discounting scheme that's going to render brokers and agents obsolete, even if it's the same article the *Times* runs every year or so.

They live in fear that Zillow might want to become a real estate broker, even though the last thing that Zillow would ever do is move from an industry with massive to minimal margins. Doubters drop their commission at the first sign of an objection, even though the services they provide are far superior to their discounting competitors. The Doubters reek of desperation, and they amplify the challenges brought by Disruptors and Discounters by becoming an echo chamber for every negative word they hear.

That's what we have to overcome as an industry: the Disruptors trying to drive us out of the business, the Discounters degrading the services we provide, and the Doubters undermining our resolve from within.

This book is about how we're going to beat them by building a better real estate industry. We're going to start by recognizing the reality that this industry is no longer the broker-centric business of the pre-1970s era, or the agent-centric business that has dominated since. Rather, the real estate industry needs to become client-centric—practicing what we'll call Client-Oriented Real Estate or CORE—focusing not on our own needs (the needs to make a sale) but on the needs of our clients for an exceptional real estate experience.

We're going to diagnose the central weakness of the real estate industry, which is what I'm going to call the original sin—this misconception that real estate agents are merely salespeople. Why is that a misconception? Because agents have tremendous responsibilities that go well beyond the role of a traditional salesperson. They need the skills, training, and support of service professionals, since most of the work they do is all about helping people buy and sell homes.

Unfortunately, because of the original sin, we've built an industry based entirely on a sales-dominant mind-set, which has undermined our public image, impaired our relationships with our clients, and even impacted the quality of the work we do.

We need to flip that mentality. We need to stop thinking about ourselves and start thinking about our clients. We need to stop trying to satisfy our own needs and start trying to satisfy theirs. It's not about us anymore. At least, we have to stop making it about us if we want to overcome the challenges of the Disruptors, Discounters, and Doubters.

The Disruptors see how we've been so obsessed with sales that we've neglected the needs of our clients and are trying to provide consumers with a better transactional experience. So how do we beat them? We disrupt ourselves by putting our innovative energies into improving client experiences rather than simply generating leads.

The Discounters see how we've allowed ourselves to be commodified as cookie-cutter salespeople and are trying to offer a superficially similar level of service for a dramatically reduced price. How do we beat them? We're going to stop making outdated claims for our value proposition and start promoting the true significance of the services we do provide.

And the Doubters? Well, the Doubters see all of this happening around them and feel powerless because in their hearts they don't see the value they provide to clients. So we either need to get them out of the business or help them understand that, at its best, the real estate industry has the potential to provide an outstanding, important service at a reasonable price. We need to help them believe in themselves.

So what I'm going to do in this book is suggest changes we need to make to adapt to a client-centric world and confront the challenges of Disruptors, Discounters, and Doubters.

Who Is the Industry?

And who exactly is *we*? I wrote this book mostly for my friends and colleagues who are real estate agents and brokers, who form the backbone of the traditional real estate industry. They're the ones on the front lines working with clients every day, who will be most impacted by any kind of major disruption to our business model.

But it's not just about them. I'm also writing for all the smart people who support the traditional real estate model of brokers and agents representing clients buying and selling properties:

- *Networks.* The franchise systems, the National Association of REALTORS®, the Realty Alliance, Leading Real Estate Companies of the World, and other broker and agent networks that provide support for those agents and brokers.

- *Consultants.* Brilliant advisors and consultants such as Victor Lund and Marilyn Wilson of the Wav group; Steve Murray of Real Trends; Marc Davison, Brian Boero, Joel Burslem, and the team at 1000 Watt; and Stefan Swanepoel, Jack Miller, Leslie Ebersole, and everyone at T3 Sixty, all of whom help brokers and agents get better.

- *Educators.* My colleagues in the training industry, not just the big coaching superstars Tom Ferry, Brian Buffini, Larry Kendall, Mike Ferry, Verl Workman, Darryl Davis, Mark Leader, and everyone else who helps agents build careers, but also all the dedicated educators working at franchise systems, brokerages, boards, and roaming the country from conference room to conference room.

- *Media.* My friends John Featherston of RIS Media and Brad Inman of Inman News, who so ably document the ups and downs of our industry.

- *Partners.* And I'm even incorporating our partners (often called vendors) who support the rest of us in helping buyers and sellers through the real estate transactional process with technology and systems that make our jobs better and easier. And, yes, that includes Zillow.

We're all in this together, regardless of the color of our sign, or our internal commission structure, or how much money we make. We all want, or should want, to build a better industry.

So let's get started.

Introduction: The Dawn of the Client-Oriented Real Estate Industry

MY MOTHER, MARSHA, NEVER SET OUT TO BE A real estate broker. She'd gone to nursing school, worked as a nurse for a year or two, met my dad, got married, had me and then my brother Greg, then stayed at home with both of us for a few years during the mid-1970s.

But she never went back to nursing. Instead, on a whim and bored taking care of two brats, she decided to get her real estate license. She worked as an agent for a few years and found she liked it and was good at it. But then she had another son, my brother Matt, and wanted more control over her schedule rather than schlep buyers around all the time. So she got her broker's license, bought into a partnership, bought out her partners, and started a company that in almost forty years has grown to over a thousand agents and $2 billion in transactional volume every year (and in the meantime had a fourth son, Dan.)

She had good timing. The real estate industry exploded in the 1970s when the baby boomers finally grew up, moved out of their parents' houses (or their communes), and realized they needed a place to live. Home starts and home sales both set records in 1971, then again the next year. More sales meant more commissions, which meant more people interested in becoming real estate agents. So we had lots of new and ambitious agents coming into the business, particularly many women like Marsha who were attracted to a career with low barriers to entry, unlimited income potential, and flexible hours.

Suddenly, real estate became a viable option for building a career, and people flocked to get their licenses: membership in the National

Association of REALTORS rose from 94,625 to 761,381 members during the 1970s, an increase of 800 percent in just ten years. Think about that. Membership in NAR right now is at about 1.2 million, so it grew more in just the 1970s than it did in the forty or so years since.

And those agents changed this industry. In the old days, the real estate business revolved around the broker, usually a Chamber of Commerce type who set up shop right on Main Street, knew everyone in town, and was the person to go to if you wanted to buy or sell property. If he or she had competitors, it was other single-agent brokerages similarly built around the skills of the owner.

That's why so many of the country's oldest and most successful real estate brokerages are named for founding partners. Go across the country: Howard Hanna in the Midwest. Baird and Warner in Chicago. Douglas Elliman in Manhattan. Long & Foster in the mid-Atlantic states. Watson Realty in Florida. Even Coldwell Banker, a franchise that was born as a San Francisco brokerage formed by Colbert Coldwell and Benjamin Arthur Banker. Those were all companies started by real live people—founding brokers who started their businesses as mostly one-person shops and built from there.

And not all of them were men. Just in my local area in the Northeast, we have any number of real estate companies founded by women, who still bear the name of that founding partner: Corcoran Real Estate in New York City, Julia B. Fee in the New York suburbs, Gloria Nilsson and Diane Turton on the New Jersey Shore.

Moreover, not all of these eponymous firms are big brokers. As you go through the small towns of this country, particularly in the Northeast where the brokerages are older, you'll probably find boutiques still named for founding partners, long after he or she retired or passed on.

Back in the day, that was the governing model for real estate brokerage: lead brokers, well-connected, wired into their local communities, handling the business themselves. But as those brokers became more successful, they realized they could not manage the increased flow of business on their own, so they took on additional salespeople to handle clients and customers generated by the lead broker. Those associates were not supposed to generate their own business—they were just supposed to follow up on the broker-owner's leads. So they only tended to get a minimal split of the commissions earned. That's where the traditional 50/50 split came from: it was a broker-centric model in which the lead broker was the star, the main source of lead development and revenue, who was thereby entitled to a large portion of the commission earned by junior associates.

This broker-centric model of real estate dominated the industry from its inception in the 1920s all the way through the 1970s: brokers as rainmakers paid out 50 percent splits to subordinate and dependent associates, running a single office on Main Street.

But that 1970s wave of new agents like Marsha created the modern real estate industry, changing the relationship between brokers and agents, spurring the development of national networks, and transforming the compensation model.

Agent Role

The agents like Marsha who came into the business in the 1970s had different goals from the traditional associates who had worked for brokers in the past. They were entrepreneurial, not ministerial; independent, not dependent. They didn't want to have to rely on brokers to generate leads. They wanted to, and expected to, build their own business within a business. They didn't want a job, they wanted careers.

Broker Role

As the agent role evolved, brokers evolved. They built larger and larger armies of agents, transforming themselves from rainmaker to manager. Many stopped working with clients altogether, so they wouldn't be competing with their productive agents. Rather, brokers took on operational and management responsibilities: providing mentoring, coaching, and training services, facilities management, technological support, accounting, and the like. If they provided lead generation, it was mostly through brand marketing, rather than personal referrals. Even broker names changed, since owners who were no longer rainmakers mostly stopped naming their brokerages after themselves. Instead, they started giving their firms independent brand identities that could more easily be blended with individual agent branding. Indeed, you rarely find large brokerages founded in the modern era that are named for their owner, such as Redfin, ZipRealty, Compass, and Realty One.

Franchising

As the broker and agent roles evolved, so did the entire industry, with the creation and expansion of national franchise systems designed to provide brokers with the systems needed to manage rapidly growing armies of agents, most of whom were founded in the 1970s or early 1980s: ERA (1971), Century 21 (1971), RE/MAX and Realty Executives (1973), the original Better Homes and Gardens (1978), Coldwell Banker (1982), and Keller Williams (1983).

The franchise systems not only provided structure for existing brokers, but they made it easy for the most enterprising of the modern real estate agents to start their own brokerages. Find an office, sign a franchise agreement, and you're in business. Indeed, that's exactly what Marsha did in the late 1970s, signing a franchise agreement to become Century 21 American Heritage.

Training

Similarly, all these agents trying to build their own businesses created an insatiable demand for training and coaching. So we also saw the development of national training organizations led by pioneers Mike Ferry, Floyd Wickman, and Tom Hopkins, all of whom started barnstorming the country in the mid-1970s to teach agents how to generate business and build their brands. I can remember Marsha bringing me to a Mike Ferry sales rally when I was a teenager in the mid-1980s, watching him stride ferociously across the stage and berating agents who were too timid to do what was needed to succeed.

Compensation Models

Of course, as the business model changed, the compensation system changed. Agents generating their own transactions weren't satisfied paying half their commissions to their broker, so new models evolved giving them a larger share of the pie—largely popularized through the 1973 founding of the RE/MAX franchise network by Dave and Gail Liniger and the Realty Executives franchise network by R. Dale Rector.

Ultimately, the 1970s revolution in the industry led to what we now think of as the agent-centric era of real estate brokerage. Agents generate their own leads. They manage their own clients. They do their own marketing. And they collect most of the commission revenue.

The Agent-Centric Era

In the thirty years since the 1970s revolution, the industry's agent-centricity has only accelerated, which has put increasing pressure on the viability and role of brokerages.

Most significantly, we've seen the further expansion of agent-centric compensation models. Keller Williams was founded in 1983, right after the 1970s revolution, but its capped company-dollar business model really took off in the 2000s, not only spurring the expansion of the brand but putting pressure on even the most traditional of full-service brokers to raise splits and pare down services and expenses.

More recently, we've seen even more aggressive agent-centric fee-based business models narrow the role of the broker even more, with brokers essentially becoming landlords who simply charge agents monthly or transactional fees in exchange for a minimal set of services.

Consequently, brokers have had to scramble to find ways to maintain financial viability. That's why so many brokers have created affiliate companies in mortgage, title, property management, and insurance in order to generate further revenue out of their client base. Indeed, some brokerages are no longer inherently viable, but are instead simply loss leaders that generate home service clients for home service businesses with the potential for meaningful profit margins.

That's also why we're seeing the rapid consolidation of the industry, with the largest, strongest firms like Home Services and NRT, and even multistate independents like Douglas Elliman and Howard Hanna, expanding through acquisition and strengthening economies of scale that allow them to remain profitable. Essentially, if you're a modern broker, you can be successful if you're a really small niche company in a narrow market where you can keep your costs down, particularly if you're a producing broker competing with your agents. Or you can be successful if you get big enough to achieve economies of scale for your operations, especially if you can build profitable affiliated businesses. But if you're a medium-sized traditional broker who depends on agents to do their own lead generation while you pick up the majority of the operational costs, you're getting squeezed.

Indeed, you can see the increasing marginalization of the broker-age role with the rising trend of agent teams, where top agents hire junior agents to represent buyers, manage listings, or make showings in return for a portion of the team leader's split. In many cases, these team leaders are taking on the traditional role of the broker, providing management, supervision, training, and lead generation for their dependent agents. But they're not becoming brokers themselves.

Ironically, agent teams are taking us full circle back to the beginnings of the industry. Think about it—these agent team leaders are basically traditional broker-centric brokers. They generate all the leads, distribute them to associate team members, pay out a portion of the split, and provide management, training, supervision, and all the rest. We tend to think of agent teams as revolutionary, but they're really just re-creating the broker-centric business model.

The difference, of course, is that these top agents aren't going out on their own and opening up their own brokerages, the way their forebears like Marsha did. Rather, instead of taking on the operational headaches and costs of running a brokerage, they're essentially building a brokerage-within-a-brokerage. Indeed, they're building a broker-centric brokerage within an agent-centric brokerage. But they don't want to be a broker; they want to be a team leader.

After all, why be a broker in an agent-centric industry?

The Client-Centric Era

So what's been missing in all of this history of the real estate industry? We had the broker-centric era. Then we had the agent-centric era.

But what about the client?

I mean, isn't it a little strange that we've always defined real estate industry eras as centering on the primacy of either the broker or the agent? And isn't it a little revealing that the signature innovation of the agent-centric era is the evolution of compensation models, which has nothing at all to do with the kinds of services we provide our clients? Whether it's about the broker or the agent, it's always been about us, not the client.

And that shows. If you look at the history of our industry, you'll see just how inattentive we've been to the needs of our clients, focused so much more intently on ourselves. Even worse, when we've had opportunities to improve the client-service experience in the industry, we haven't embraced them—we've fought them. We fought against sharing listings with other brokers. We fought against providing representational services to buyers. And ultimately, we fought desperately to preserve our gatekeeper role to control consumer access to real estate information. Why? Because we've been blindly and mindlessly industry-centric.

But even if we don't want to acknowledge it, our industry has been changing around us. We can trace the slow empowering of the real estate client all the way back to the rise of multiple listing systems in the middle of the last century. Before the MLS, consumers were at the mercy of the broker who had control of the local inventory, like a car buyer who had to visit a particular dealership if she wanted a specific car. In many cases, buyers couldn't choose their broker—they had to work with whoever had exclusively listed the house they wanted. That changed, of course, with MLS reciprocity, which allowed consumers to work with a broker or agent of their choice, who could show them virtually any home for sale on the market.

This consumer freedom to choose an agent expanded about twenty-five years ago with the emergence of buyer agency throughout the country. Before buyer agency, all the agents worked for the seller, so consumers would end up working with and forming relationships with agents who didn't actually represent them. With buyer agency, though, buyers could not only get an agent of their choice but also get the benefit of fiduciary representation throughout their transaction.

Consumer empowerment really accelerated, though, with the popularization of the internet, especially when consumers no longer had to go through broker and agent gatekeepers to find out what homes were for sale in their neighborhood. Real estate inventory search came to the internet in the late 1990s and exploded after the internet data-exchange protocols were developed in 2000. And right from the beginning, the traditional real estate industry ceded control of internet search.

NAR had the opportunity to create a consumer facing website that would have possibly preserved that gatekeeper role for brokers and agents, but they outsourced the responsibility for Realtor.com to third-party developers, effectively birthing the third-party portal, inadvertently expanding consumer choices and ultimately paving the way for search dominance by sites such as Zillow and Trulia—rather than by brokers or agents. You can argue about whether that was a good or bad thing for the industry, but it was clearly a good thing for expanding consumer choice.

But it's not just about search. One of the central tenets of internet technology is that information wants to be free, and we've seen how dramatic increases in the amount and quality of real estate information that's become available to consumers has continually empowered the consumer at the expense of brokers and agents:

Marketing. Go back twenty-five years when brokers and agents dominated the newspaper, which was the primary vehicle for advertising real estate. Then, when inventory went online, we still controlled how listings were marketed through distribution channels. Now, with most MLS systems providing automatic listing syndication to nearly every site available, few brokers or agents maintain active control over their own listing distribution.

Valuation. Consumers used to go to agents and brokers to find out how much their home is worth. The Zestimate changed that, obviously. Now, even though brokerage and agent websites often provide competing valuations, they're no longer the perceived authority.

Sold information. Even as consumers gained access to information about what homes were for sale, they still had to go to brokers and agents to find information about sold homes. But that has started to change as well, as more websites are providing public record sold data, and even MLS sold data, to complement their listing aggregation.

Agent Ratings and Reviews. Until recently, consumers had no way of knowing whether that nice agent they met at an open house was any good at her job. Now, virtually every agent in the business has an online "report card" of ratings and reviews, which, while imperfect, do empower consumers to become more selective when hiring an agent.

Agent Performance. Consumers are getting even more leverage over the agent and broker selection process as websites start to provide production statistics like "number of homes sold" and performance analytics like "average sales price," "days-on-market," or "listing success rate," all of which allow consumers to choose their agent based on their track record.

It's not just real estate—the internet empowered consumers in all sorts of industries. But increasing transparency has hit the real estate industry particularly hard, precisely because we clung desperately to this industry-centric view that depended on our ability to maintain control over the consumer's access to real estate information. And we fought every step of the way. We fought to keep the inventory off-line. We fought ratings. We fought access to sold information. And we're still fighting over performance analytics. But information wants to be free, and our command of the industry should not, and cannot, rely on our control over that information.

The industry is already client-centric. The consumer is already in charge. We just haven't adapted. We're still acting as if we're in control: like we're the gatekeepers of information, like we have a monopoly on listing marketing, like clients absolutely have to come to us to buy or sell property, like we have the luxury to still spend all our time finding creative ways to split the commission pie. We're still focusing on our own needs, rather than doing anything to improve our product by making the real estate transactional experience better. We're still offering the same value proposition that we did thirty years ago, when Marsha and her colleagues kept the real estate inventory on index cards hidden in shoe boxes. We're still acting as if buyers and sellers don't have any other options, when they do.

Indeed, we sometimes don't even think of our clients as our clients! I can't tell you how many times I've heard brokers at conferences say something like, "Buyers and sellers aren't my clients, my clients are my agents!"

Think about that. The agent-centric model has so taken over our mind-set that many brokers no longer see themselves as having relationships with their actual clients. Instead, they're built around providing services that attend to the needs of the agents affiliated with them.

Now, I'm not saying we should go back to the broker-centric days of 50/50 splits, where agents were subordinate to lead brokers. That's not my point. But we need to recognize the potential consequences when broker-owners no longer see themselves as responsible for and accountable to the actual clients of the firm. How are we going to adapt to a client-centric world and improve the service experience we're providing, if we don't even see our clients as our clients?

It's not just that the "agents are my clients" perspective puts brokers in a mind-set that disclaims responsibility for the service experience they provide. It's the practical reality that too many brokers are simultaneously cutting back on expenses that pay for the very services that help agents provide consumers with better experiences. They can't afford to pay for training or coaching that would help agents become better at their actual jobs. They can't afford to pay for management guidance to assist agents in facilitating clients through difficult transactions. They can't afford to pay for operational support to take some logistical burdens off agents and allow them to focus on providing a better service experience.

You could argue that it doesn't make a difference, that if brokers cut back on those services to pay a higher split, then agents will simply pay for them out of their extra income. Certainly, that's the assumption underlying the extreme broker-as-landlord model—that agents will invest their money more efficiently on the client-service experience than their broker would.

But can you think of any industry that decentralizes accountability for providing its central consumer experience? Can you think of any successful company that puts the entire responsibility for delivering quality service to the point-of-sale provider without any real training, management guidance, or operational support? Even assuming that agents are willing or able to replicate those services out of their own pockets, how is that more economically efficient?

In most businesses, you want to build economies of scale that allow you to provide services to larger groups of people at a cheaper per-person cost. How do we create those efficiencies if we shirk the costs of improving the client-service experience to individual agents? And how is it more logistically efficient for an agent to take on operational responsibilities that detract from the time she has to put into generating or servicing clients? If anything, this decentralization of responsibility for the consumer experience makes it even harder to improve the level of service we're providing in our industry.

Let me be clear: I don't blame the agents on this. Naturally, they want splits to be as high as possible. I get it. But I think that most responsible agents understand that the brokerage needs to retain enough company dollars to pay for the services that are necessary to help agents do their job for the client. And I think that most of them recognize that the brokerage needs to make a modest profit on the business to justify the commitment that those brokers make and the risks they take. It's up to the brokers to make sure that they're efficiently providing only those services that the agents value and that are necessary to service our mutual clients' needs.

Even more importantly, brokers need to do a much better job of articulating their value, like an agent in a listing presentation answering commission objections, so they're not always competing on price. If brokers don't, then they're going to continue to be marginalized—or driven out of business. And they'll deserve it.

But all that starts with brokers recognizing that their actual clients are the buyers and sellers paying all of them thousands of dollars for each transaction. Agents don't need to be clients to be valued. They're vital precisely because they're on the front lines delivering services directly to the clients. All industries depend on a talented, productive, and motivated workforce to be successful. Indeed, companies become legendary precisely because of the quality of the people that work for them: Nordstrom. Disney. Apple. Starbucks. The Four Seasons. But that doesn't mean that those companies think of their employees as their clients. Rather, they became legendary because they value their employees and empower them with the tools, training, and resources to attend to the needs of their actual clients: the people who buy their products.

So, yes, it's important for brokers to think about the needs of their agents, precisely because agents are the delivery system for services to the client. And if you want to be poetic and say "I treat all my agents like they're my clients" as a means of articulating a message that you value your agents and want them to be happy and motivated, that's fine.

But in an increasingly client-centric world, we should never forget that the clients of the brokerage are, indeed, the actual clients. And that we need to focus on their needs, not on our own.

So What Does It Take?

This is what I call Client-Oriented Real Estate or CORE—the concept that we need to be focused on our clients, and their needs, rather than on ourselves and our own needs. Success is not about brokers. It's not about agents. It's about clients and how we can provide them with a better real estate experience.

Here's an example of what I mean. For years, real estate agents recognized that homeowners wanted to keep track of the value of their home. But instead of focusing on their need (that is, "What is my home worth?"), we prioritized our own need—the need to generate a listing lead. So on every piece of marketing we ever created, we advertised an offer for a "Free CMA!"

And what was the "Free CMA!"? Basically, a chance to sit through a listing presentation. We figured that anyone calling on the offer was probably at least thinking about selling, so we used the "Free CMA!" ad as a way of getting in the door. Then, before actually answering the question, we launched into our twenty-seven-point marketing plan. Why? Because it wasn't about their need, it was about our need.

And what happened next? The Zestimate happened next. The smart people at Zillow figured out a clever way to actually service that need, with an online valuation that homeowners could access in just a few clicks. Now, we all know that the Zestimate was wildly inaccurate, and mostly clickbait, but at least Zillow was trying to service the need. Indeed, they started servicing the need without a firm idea of how they would monetize the service. But they eventually figured it out, didn't they?

We abused our clients' needs. Zillow serviced them and subsequently built a billion-dollar company and one of the premier brands in real estate.

Zillow gave us a lesson we still haven't learned. If we don't pay attention to what your clients need, someone else will. If we don't adapt our value proposition, someone else will provide something better. If we're so focused on the short term that we neglect to make investments in the future, someone else will steal our future out from under us.

So how do we stop that from happening? We start focusing on our clients and what they need. The CORE formula is simple: think expansively about what our clients need, think creatively about how we can service that need, and then execute.

So what do our clients need, and what changes do we need to make to service them well?

They need agents who act as service professionals who are dedicated to solving their problems, not salespeople who are just trying to get them to buy something. So we need to change the way we think about what we do.

They need agents who are smart at their jobs, who will give people an amazing experience in buying and selling a home. So we need to make changes in the way we hire and train agents and in the systems and tools we provide them.

Buyers and sellers need an industry that doesn't rely on an outdated value proposition based on the gatekeeper mentality of twenty-five years ago. So we need to change our approach to articulating the services we provide our clients and overcome the "all agents are the same" mentality we've helped create.

Our clients need an easier and faster real estate transaction than the mess that they go through now. So we have to find ways to simplify the process of buying and selling a home, to help give our clients a better experience and fend off the challenges of Disruptors who are promising that simpler transaction.

Finally, they need, and we need, people in this industry who believe in themselves and in the value of what they do. So we have to change our attitude and stop doubting ourselves.

I offer five key changes—the changes we need to make to create a client-centric world if we want to overcome the challenges we face from Disruptors, Discounters, and Doubters.

Key #1: Stop Thinking Like (Just) a Salesperson

A FEW YEARS AGO, I WAS TOYING with the idea of buying a second home on the New Jersey Shore. I had money saved up from the sale of some real estate in Manhattan. I was in the process of having my first kid, and I believed that vacation home values had declined to the point that they were becoming smart investments.

So at night I would pull out my iPad and check out the listings on Zillow, the same way that so many buyers play around looking at homes. Shopping for real estate online is one of the great ways to while away your time on the internet, probably just behind snooping on your exes on Facebook.

But I didn't start working with an agent. Why? Because I was still basically window-shopping. I wasn't sure I was going to buy something, and I was reluctant to waste an agent's time on what might have been a passing fancy. Moreover, I was confident that I could find what I needed by looking online, even though I didn't know a whole lot about the market. After all, I was an experienced real estate professional: I know how to comparison shop and how to read a market, and I figured I could save everyone a lot of time if I invested some effort in looking on my own before retaining an agent. At least, that's what I told myself.

So I probably spent a few months shopping second homes up and down the Shore. I'd be on that tablet for hours at night, saving properties and clicking through pictures, obsessing over the slightest details, and chasing rabbit holes for municipal information about homes I found interesting.

And then I hired an agent and realized how much valuable Facebook-stalking time I'd frittered away because I'd wasted all that time looking online. In just one brief conversation, that agent clued me in to all the subtleties of the market that I had absolutely no way of learning just from looking at pictures and descriptions of homes online—the areas that held value over time, which towns were probably too honky-tonk for me, the importance of certain construction features, the amenities that were crucial for maintaining high rental values.

I learned more in a half-hour conversation with him than I'd gleaned from three months of looking by myself. And when I sent him my list of favorites from the app, he immediately discounted about 90 percent of them: properties with bad layouts, small lots, suspect mechanicals, and all the problems that aren't highlighted in those charming descriptions.

The difference in the properties I pulled for myself and the ones that he selected for me was stark, and the reason was simple: he knew the market, and he had seen the properties. He knew what I needed a lot better than I did.

And that's just the beginning of the experience. He hadn't even started all the work that would go into guiding me through reviewing the inventory, selecting the right home, negotiating a deal, and helping me through the entire transaction. This was just the tip of the iceberg, but already it was clear how much value that agent was bringing to the process.

Moreover, my experience is not unique. If you're a real estate agent, you know how hard you have to work, and how much you need to know, to help a client through a real estate transaction. If you're working with a buyer, you not only have to know the market and be able to quickly ascertain what a client needs, but you then have to help that client through the long and difficult process of sifting through the inventory, finding the right home to buy, and shepherding the buyer through the transaction.

That means countless hours of schlepping the buyer from home to home, staying on top of changes in the market, and then schlepping to even more homes. And even when you find the right home, you have to visit it two, three, four, or more times to make sure it's really the right one, sometimes taking all the extended family who want to weigh in on the decision. Then comes all the work putting together the transaction: the offers, the counteroffers, the inspections, dealing with attorneys or escrow agents, doing grunt work for the mortgage brokers. It's a staggering amount of work.

It's the same for listing agents working with a seller. You have to analyze the market, pull comps, and then experience the never-ending joy of explaining to a seller why his home is worth a lot less than he thought. Then if you even get the listing, your real work starts: taking and uploading pictures and videos, writing property descriptions, preparing marketing material, checking property data, doing all the data entry for the MLS, and trying to explain to the seller why his standards of clean and neat are not necessarily universal. And once the property is on the market, it's endless open houses, chasing buyer agents for feedback, and keeping the seller updated about everything. Then if you do get an offer, it's all the transactional work: offers, counteroffers, inspections, attorneys, and so on.

I remember getting off the phone with my Jersey Shore agent and shaking my head, ruefully realizing that I'd foolishly fallen into the same trap as so many real estate buyers. I had wasted a ton of time looking by myself instead of just letting a professional guide me. It was a valuable lesson to learn and a refreshing reminder to someone who should have known better.

The more I thought about it, though, the more I wondered why I was so reluctant to hire an agent. I had told myself at the time that it was because I was a nice person who didn't want to waste a professional agent's time when I was still just shopping. I told myself that I knew enough to shop intelligently on my own.

But I was lying to myself. The reason I didn't call an agent was simple: I didn't want to deal with a salesperson. I spent years teaching agents about prospecting and wasn't so eager to have all those techniques used on me: constant follow-up calls, drip campaigns, pressure to go out on a buyer tour. I didn't want to be a lead.

That's kind of nuts, right? I grew up in a real estate family. I got my license when I was eighteen. I've worked in the industry full-time for almost twenty years. I know thousands of real estate agents. I love the industry and believe in its value. And even I was afraid of the prospect of working with a salesperson.

If I felt that way, imagine how the average consumer thinks. But if you're an agent, you see this distrust every single day. Open house visitors who run away from you like you're carrying the plague. Buyers who refuse to come to your office, but instead want to meet "at the house." Sellers who think you're just trying to underprice their home for a quick sale. Online inquiries who don't want to give you their mobile number. Potential clients who hang up the phone when you call or ignore your well-intentioned emails. They're all scared of us.

Something has gone terribly wrong in the real estate industry. Rather than building a profession that attracts clients with the crucial services we provide, we've created a monstrosity that scares away the very people we need to attract.

Why? Because we've built this entire industry based on a total misconception of the role of the real estate agent.

To wit: real estate agents aren't *salespeople*.

If you're a real estate agent, I know that seems crazy, because people have always told you that you're in sales. You go to sales meetings and sales conventions where you get sales awards for all the sales you made. Indeed, in most states, the government says that you're a licensed real estate salesperson, a designation that you have to put on your business cards and in all your ads. And we all know that the government never gets anything wrong!

But you're not a salesperson. At least, you're not just a salesperson.

Here's why. When we call someone a salesperson, we're talking about someone who has a specific role in a business: sell stuff. If you're a salesperson, your job is to sell your company's stuff to people, so they buy your stuff rather than someone else's stuff. But that's all you do. You don't make the stuff. You don't fix the stuff. You don't help people use the stuff. You just sell the stuff. And once you sell the stuff to someone, you move on to sell it to the next person.

So when you're a salesperson, you don't have any responsibility for the product or service you're selling. For example, a car salesman helps you buy a car, but he's not the guy you call when you start seeing smoke come out of the engine. An advertising sales executive pitches clients, but she's not the one who actually writes copy or films a commercial. An electronics store sales clerk will help you choose a flat-screen television, but he's not going to schlep it over to your home to mount it on your wall.

Most industries are like that—they separate out sales and service into two discrete roles. They recognize that sales are so important, and require such specialized skills, that they need designated salespeople to ensure constant new client and customer development. Salespeople canvass for their own leads, cultivate connections, build referral networks, and give presentations to potential clients. So they need a special set of skills: the ability to talk to people, to be persuasive, to build long-term relationships, and to be persistent in the face of rejection.

But these salespeople don't have any other responsibilities after the point of sale. Why? Usually, because they'd be terrible at it. You don't want that car salesman tinkering with your engine, or that ad executive filming your commercial, or that sales clerk nailing a TV bracket into your wall. They're not trained for it, and they're probably not all that good at it.

Moreover, if you're running the business, and you've got well-trained salespeople, you don't want them distracted by all the work that goes into servicing an account or creating a product. You want them focused like a laser on selling your stuff.

That's why most businesses have what we'll call a handoff, like when a quarterback hands the ball off to a running back. Quarterbacks are good at throwing the ball, but you don't want them lunging into the line and taking hits from three-hundred-pound linemen. You want them focusing on what they do best.

Similarly, most salespeople do a handoff when they turn their clients over to the service professionals who are going to manage that client's experience—the car mechanics, the ad creative team, the TV installers. Those jobs are just as important as sales, but they require quite different skill sets. Service professionals need to be problem solvers with transaction management and communication skills: people who can figure out what clients and customers need and service those needs. They take the handoff from the salesperson and actually provide the service that's being sold.

As a real estate agent, you see this handoff every day. In the mortgage industry, for example, lenders rely on dedicated loan officers to generate the business, and specialized teams of processors to manage and underwrite the loan. In reality, loan officers are mortgage salespeople who canvass real estate agents for leads, build relationships with potential borrowers, manage the inventory of loans, and persuade people to fill out loan applications. But once the borrower fills out that application, the loan officer gets to do the handoff—giving the file to a processor responsible for reviewing the application, gathering all the necessary documents, handling clearance issues, and submitting the file for underwriting. The loan officer will often stay involved in the process to manage the client's relationship, but the back office handles the real service work.

You see the same handoff with most of the other players involved in a real estate transaction. Title and escrow, home warranty, home insurance—they all have a dedicated sales force responsible for generating business, often by canvassing real estate agents. But those sales professionals don't create title reports, close escrow, or handle warranty and insurance claims. Rather, they do the handoff of that work to trained service professionals.

But that's not what you do, is it? I mean, wouldn't it be fantastic if you could have a handoff like that? Think of all the time you'd save if you could sign a seller to a listing agreement and then let someone else take care of all the responsibilities of staging the home, creating the marketing, handling offers, and managing the transaction through to closing. Or how about if you could sign a buyer to a representation agreement, go to the office, hand it in, and then let your service department do all the screening of properties, all the showings, and then guide that client from offer to closing? You'd have all the time in the world to go out and look for new business if you didn't actually have to, you know, *do your actual job of helping clients buy and sell houses.*

It's not just the handoff. The idea that real estate agents are just salespeople is completely inconsistent with what you actually do all day. If you're like most real estate agents, you spend most of your time servicing client needs, not trying to sell them. Yes, you do a lot of work in the sales part of your job: canvassing for new clients, contacting your sphere, making pitch presentations, and so on. But most of your time is probably spent taking care of the clients you already have: the marketing and staging for your sellers, screening and showings for your buyers, and then guiding your clients from negotiation to accepted offer to closing. That's a lot of work, and it has absolutely nothing to do with sales.

You're not a salesperson just because you're involved in the sale of real estate. So is a mortgage lender, but we don't think of him as a mortgage salesperson. So is a real estate attorney, but we don't call her a legal salesperson. Lots of professionals are involved in the sale of goods or services without becoming salespeople.

Just look at investment bankers on Wall Street. Their whole job is helping a company go through the process of going public, which basically means packaging the company for sale to investors. But they're not called salespeople. Indeed, everyone who works in the financial industry is basically involved in sales in one way or another, but the only true salespeople in the industry are the ones whose specific role is to pitch clients on buying products—and who generally have absolutely no role in developing those products or managing the client's accounts. The fact that as a real estate agent you're involved in the *sale* of a property doesn't necessarily make you a *salesperson*.

Even more importantly, how can you be a salesperson if half your work is representing buyers? Salespeople always work for the seller, the person who has stuff to sell—their sole job is to persuade someone to buy their stuff instead of someone else's stuff. Is that what you do when you take out a buyer to look at homes? Are you going to try to convince them to buy your listing, or your friend's listing, or your broker's listing? Do you really care what they buy? No, you just want to make sure they buy the best home for their needs. Of course, you want them to buy something—anything!—with you as their agent, so you can make a living, but you don't really care *what* they buy.

Indeed, the idea that real estate agents are salespeople is completely inconsistent with the modern approach to buyer agency.

When you represent buyers, you're probably almost always acting in a fiduciary capacity, with a series of duties that include loyalty and confidentiality. Essentially, you need to look out for their best interests, rather than your own. How does that square with you being a salesperson? I can't think of any industry where the salesperson works for the buyer. Can you imagine the dynamic of buying a car if that salesperson worked for you, rather than for the car company? Or going to a retail store and having a fiduciary representative help you make your purchase? It just doesn't happen.

That's why I say real estate agents aren't salespeople. When we call someone a salesperson, we're usually referring to a specific type of role: a specialist whose job is to generate clients, but who has little responsibility for actually providing the service to those clients. Real salespeople get to do the handoff to service professionals; they spend the vast majority of their time on sales-related activities; and they never, ever represent buyers. That's not what you do.

Listen, I'm not just playing semantic games here. The misconception that real estate agents are just salespeople, when they have significant responsibilities to provide service to their clients, has had enormous consequences for this industry.

For example, that's probably why you feel so overwhelmed sometimes—you're doing two jobs! You're constantly switching gears from one role to the next. You come in one morning planning on doing some canvassing for new business opportunities, and a client calls you with a deal problem that takes you off course for the rest of the day. Or you're in the middle of showing a home, and you have to excuse yourself to respond to a text message with an online lead that you'll lose if you don't respond immediately.

These conflicting obligations are a constant distraction that robs you of the focus you need to do either job well. You're always juggling different colored balls in the air—a listing that needs new pictures or a price adjustment, a marketing campaign you need to mail out to your sphere, a call you have to return with problems from an inspection, and so on.

On top of that, you have to master two entirely different skill sets. You need the drive, persuasiveness, and enthusiasm of a professional salesperson who has to tirelessly campaign for new business, maintain relationships, and resist dejection-by-rejection. But you also need to maintain the skills required for a service professional: the ability to counsel and advise a client, negotiate deals, facilitate paperwork, and manage the transactional process. And you have to do all that in a competitive and complicated environment with constantly evolving technologies, an enormous and ever-changing inventory, and rapidly fluctuating market conditions.

That's why all those other industries separate out the sales and service roles, creating specialties that allow professionals to focus on a particular discipline and a limited set of responsibilities. Can you imagine the loan officers you know trying to process their own files, cutting short their canvassing in your office so that they could track down a missing tax form? And their processors would probably do an awful job managing their extensive paperwork burdens if they had to constantly run out to chat you up at a brokers' open house or respond to a prequalification request. In the mortgage business, loan officers get to focus on generating their business, and loan processors get to focus on closing the files. Both jobs are hard, but they'd be a lot tougher if one person had to do both of them.

Indeed it's almost criminally misleading to tell agents that they are just salespeople and then also ask them to manage their clients' needs through a brutally complicated transactional process. Anyone in the business knows that those are two full-time jobs and that it's tough to do them both well.

Even worse, we give agents these two difficult jobs to do, and then we only provide them with the training, support, and systems to do one of them—the sales role. And that's really the problem with this misconception that real estate agents are salespeople. Although we always pay lip service to the idea that agents are entrepreneurs, that they own a small business, we've built an industry that treats them as if their only responsibility is to generate sales. Our training, our technology, our business systems—they're all designed to cater to the agent's role as a salesperson.

Consequently, we've never built the infrastructure to support the work that agents actually do every day: helping people buy and sell homes. We don't provide the training we need to help agents learn how to give unmatched client service. We haven't built the systems we need to make it easier for agents to shoulder the dual burdens of both the sales and service roles. We've never created the technology we need to simplify the real estate transaction, to ensure that our clients have a better experience. All our energy, money, and innovation have gone to one thing: sales.

Why? Because we only think of agents as salespeople.

Now, let me be clear: None of this is a knock on salespeople. I love salespeople. Salespeople are crucial to any business enterprise. Indeed, salespeople are so important that most businesses are smart enough to focus them entirely on sales, rather than burden them with the obligations of servicing a client's needs. Salespeople are wonderful.

But you're not one of them.

And that misconception, this idea that real estate agents are just salespeople, has had an enormously negative impact on our industry.

Our Public Image

It's not easy to find a true salesperson anymore.

You won't find one, say, at an Apple store. Yet the people who work there are basically salespeople who are supposed to get you to buy an iPhone, an iPad, a computer, or some pricey accessories. But they're not called salespeople. They're called geniuses. Or, as Apple prefers, genii.

Similarly, you won't find a salesperson at Starbucks, which popularized the term *barista* to avoid having *sales clerks* behind the counter.

And you won't find one at Tesla Motors, right now the most valuable car company in the country, which has customer experience specialists rather than the stereotypical car salesmen.

Indeed, most companies have abandoned the *s*-word in titling the people who generate the sales for their businesses. Just look around your office. Do you see mortgage salespeople canvassing for leads, meeting clients, and generating sales for their lenders? No, instead, you see loan officers. Like they should be carrying some sort of shiny badge!

Try this out. Go run a search on a job listing website like Indeed. com or Monster.com for "sales" and see how many euphemisms you can come up with. You'll find account representatives and business consultants and relationship managers. Even if the word *sales* creeps into the description, you'll find it paired with more substantial-sounding titles to give it some polish, such as sales executive or vice-president of sales or sales director. Never just salesperson.

Basically, companies will say anything to avoid calling their sales force that stigmatized term *salespeople*. Why? Because most people have stereotypically negative associations that make them skeptical and suspicious of someone they perceive as a salesperson. They see a salesperson as a wily and manipulative huckster who will say or do anything to close a sale and who will pressure them to trick them into making a hasty and bad decision. They've all had bad experiences with the hard sell, and they immediately and instinctively put their guard up when working with a salesperson. People love buying, but they hate being sold—including people like me, when I was looking for a home at the Jersey Shore.

Even the positive stereotypes about salespeople carry a darker meaning. When we call someone a "natural-born salesman," we say it almost as a warning, like "watch out for him!" Or think about what the highest stereotypical compliment you can pay to a salesperson: "He could sell snow to the Eskimos." In other words, he's really terrific at getting people to buy something that they don't actually need. And that's what makes him great! But is that what you want when you're thinking of buying something? Someone who is really good at getting you to buy stuff that you don't need?

And yet, that's the perception we create when we call real estate agents "salespeople." Unlike all these other industries, we virtually embrace the term. Often, it's our legal designation. It's how people describe us and how we describe ourselves. And that, by itself, causes much of the negative perception of the real estate industry.

Just look at public opinion surveys measuring what consumers think of real estate agents. For example, a 2013 poll by Google Consumer Surveys asked over 1,000 adults a simple question: "Do you trust real estate agents?" Over 67 percent of the respondents, over two-thirds of them, said no.

Consider the annual Gallup survey that rates the honesty and ethics of professions by measuring public opinion about a variety of professionals. The survey asks respondents: "How you would rate the honesty and ethical standards of people in these different fields—very high, high, average, low, or very low?"

Again, the results were a little depressing. For one thing, significantly more people said that real estate agents had "low or very low" honesty and ethical standards (25%) than "high or very high" standards (20%). The rest had us at "average." That's bad. Even worse, though, here are some of the professions that people think have higher ethical and honesty standards than we do: building contractors, lawyers, bankers, and journalists. I mean, bankers almost destroyed the world's economy a few years ago, and they're more ethical and honest than we are?

Indeed, what you notice when you look at that table of results is that sales-oriented professions tend to fall to the bottom: advertising practitioners, car salespeople, telemarketers, and lobbyists.

People just don't have a lot of trust in the integrity and honesty of salespeople.

The only good news is that we finished above Members of Congress! Yay?

You can also see these negative public perceptions in the way that pop culture portrays real estate agents in movies and television as fast-talking hucksters. Take, for example, the most famous motivational sales talk in history: the Alec Baldwin "coffee is for closers" speech in *Glengarry Glen Ross*, in which he berates a group of hapless real estate salespeople for failing to get the "good leads" to "sign on the line that is dotted." Or the famous episode of the *Simpsons* when Marge Simpson failed as a real estate agent because she couldn't effectively lie to her clients by, say, describing a house literally on fire as having a motivated seller.

Also consider an ad a few years ago for a mobile company, which showed "Ronnie Briskman, Motivated Realtor," a stereotypical real estate agent in a badge and blazer fast-talking into her mobile phone, reeling off these gems:

It's a sprawling ranch—do you like ranching?
Any closet is a walk-in closet if you try hard enough.
That third fire might have been arson, but that kid's going to prison.
Sylvia, hi! Who's my big seller?
Someone here is a big seller!
I'm going to tell you "it's a buyer's market."
"It is a seller's market, baby!"
Hello, hold on, who are you?
If a celebrity dies in your house, that's a landmark!

What's particularly scary about this commercial is that the mobile company wasn't trying to convince us that this real estate agent was a duplicitous shill, telling some people it's a seller's market and other people it's a buyer's market. They just figured people already knew that and used that presumption as a jumping-off point for the gag. Why? Because she's a salesperson, and that's what salespeople do.

Even worse, people don't even take salespeople seriously. Consider, for example, how real estate agents escaped most of the blame for the collapse of the market in the past decade. Yes, agents were criticized and mocked for their eternal "it's a great time to buy" mantras that facilitated the over-exuberant market. But when the market ultimately crashed, people blamed bankers for their lax credit standards, Wall Street for creating the appetite for securitized mortgages, the Federal Reserve for keeping interest rates too low, and even the government for its failure to properly regulate the mortgage industry. But few people held the real estate agents or the brokerage industry accountable for the collapse of their investment class, mainly because no one took us seriously enough to give us that kind of responsibility.

Now, I'm not necessarily disappointed that the real estate bubble debacle did not result in people like me appearing before Senate sub-committees to explain ourselves and fight off a whole bunch of new regulations. But it's honestly a little insulting that everyone involved in real estate came under the microscope except for the very people who are involved in helping people buy and sell houses.

You would think that if you helped someone make an investment that ultimately turned out to be a disaster, you would shoulder some of the blame. But we didn't. Why? Because you don't generally blame salespeople for the performance of the product they sell. We didn't get credit when the market went up, and we didn't get blame when the market went down because we're not considered serious profession-als. We're considered salespeople who have no more responsibility for the product they sell than a guy hawking sedans at a used car lot.

The real estate industry isn't blind to the implications created by the word *salesperson*. But the substitutes we use are often inexact or clunky. For example, real estate agents in Manhattan call them-selves brokers, which is technically incorrect since most of them are licensed as salespeople working under their actual broker's license. But it definitely sounds better. Indeed, although I use the term *real estate agents* throughout this book, the word *agent* itself is a little mis-leading because it actually refers narrowly to the agency relationship between a client and a real estate professional. We talk about a broker having real estate agents, but they're not actually the broker's agents; they're the agents of buyers and sellers. That can get confusing, so I try not to think about it too hard.

The word REALTOR®, of course, is a much more neutral way of describing a real estate agent that also has some professional cachet, but the NAR has put so many restrictions on its use that many of us shy away from employing it in our everyday interactions.

Technically, it only refers to members of the National Association of REALTORS, but that alone would not be that constrictive since most agents in the country are actually members. Yet NAR, in its understandable but thoroughly frustrating attempt to protect the trademark, makes it incredibly burdensome to actually use the term when describing agents—officially, you have to put it in all caps, as I have here, and add the trademark designation, and you can't use it in any descriptive way that would set you apart from other members of the association. It's a much better term with more professional connotations than salesperson, but it's also a lot of bother.

No matter how we slice it, though, real estate agents are thought of as salespeople. It's the most common descriptive term; it's what most states call us; and it's what's officially on our business cards. And that, by itself, has had a tremendous impact on the way people perceive us.

Client Relationships

These stereotypically negative associations aren't just a public image problem. Rather, they have an enormous impact on our ability to generate a trusting relationship with our clients. Even though we have basically the same types of fiduciary duties that attorneys have to their clients, we rarely get the same level of trust. Why? Because clients still think of us as salespeople, not as someone legally required to act in their best interests.

Think about some of the challenges you face in building a strong, trusting relationship with your clients. You're at that open house where the visitors scurry away from you when you ask them to sign in. You've gotten a call from a potential buyer who just wanted to meet at the house rather than come in to talk to you beforehand. These people are so afraid to establish a relationship with an agent because they're scared of getting involved with a salesperson who they think will start pressuring them to buy something.

Or consider about how hard it is to build trust with a seller. How many times have you presented a strong, accurate CMA only to have the seller completely reject it and price the home well above the established market value? How many deals have you lost because sellers wouldn't listen to you and turned down a series of reasonable offers on their home? Too many sellers simply don't trust our advice because they're reflexively suspicious of a salesperson who they think just wants to make a quick and profitable sale.

You don't see this kind of skepticism with other professionals. Before I started working full-time for my family's real estate company, I was a litigation attorney with a big Manhattan law firm, and I was in the room dozens of times to watch lawyers counsel their clients about accepting or rejecting offers of settlement. In virtually all those cases, I saw clients accept their attorney's recommendations without complaint. I never, ever saw the kind of client skepticism and suspicion that I see every day in the real estate industry.

And it's not just attorneys. Lots of other service professionals and small-business owners develop far more trusting relationships with their customers and clients than we do. People don't suspect doctors of ordering procedures because they get extra fees for them. People don't think their electricians are suggesting a rewiring project because they need the work. People don't worry that their hairdressers are only recommending a particular style because it allows them to charge more. Why do all these professionals generate more trust than we do? Because their customers and clients don't see them as salespeople.

That's the impact of what I refer to here as the original sin. No matter how many times we explain to our clients that we're their agent representing their best interests, and no matter how many forms we give them explaining our fiduciary duties, they still see us as salespeople. And because of that, they don't trust us.

Building Our Business

Indeed, the original sin even impacts the way our *potential* clients see us. For years, real estate trainers like the great Brian Buffini have preached the gospel of the personal referral as the foundation for building your career. And they're right. But generating referral business is particularly hard when people think of you as a salesperson.

Think of it this way: Why don't lawyers have salespeople? After all, law firms need clients, just like real estate brokerages do. And it's not just law firms. Doctors, dentists, architects, accountants, funeral directors, interior decorators, hair stylists, engineers, contractors, plumbers, electricians, mechanics—whether they are white collar or blue collar, whether they operate out of an office or a shop or even their own basement, few service-oriented businesses have designated salespeople to canvass for clients or customers.

Moreover, those professionals don't seem to spend a lot of their time running around prospecting and canvassing for new business. They usually have basic sales skills needed to convince potential clients and customers of their reliability and competence, and they might do some advertising, but they don't take on nearly the same burdens of the traditional sales role that real estate agents do.

So if they don't have designated salespeople, and they don't do sales themselves, how do service professionals who run their own small businesses generate most of their clients?

The answer is simple: they get significant word-of-mouth personal referral business based on the quality of the work they do.

It's not just the quality of the work they do—it's the type of work they do. Most service professionals can rely on that referral business precisely because consumers tend to look for personal recommendations when they need to hire a professional to do highly specialized work that requires specific expertise. For example, if we need someone to rewire our home, or write our will, or heal our illness, or cut our hair, we're likely to ask our friends and colleagues for a referral. Why? Because we recognize that a good practitioner can make a big difference over someone who is merely mediocre.

So when it comes to important, complicated work, we recognize that a skilled practitioner makes a difference, and so we do our due diligence: we look for a referral, we listen for the word of mouth, we work hard to find the right person. Indeed, I've never known a woman who would go into a hair salon and take the "up person."

That's why business owners who provide professional services don't need salespeople and don't need to prospect—because they generate a steady flow of word-of-mouth referrals based on the quality of the work they do. Lawyers who win cases, plumbers who clear pipes, architects who build beautiful buildings, hair stylists who give precision cuts, accountants who save you money while keeping you out of jail—their work sells itself. Indeed, these service professionals have a strong incentive to hone their craft, to become proficient at their jobs, because they know they'll eventually be rewarded with repeat and referral business. They might advertise, they might market themselves a bit to get the word out there, but they don't have salespeople.

But real estate agents have a much harder time generating that same steady flow of personal referrals. Why? Because consumers perceive real estate agents as salespeople and don't think to search for referrals for a salesperson. Indeed, why would they spend a lot of time trying to find a "good agent" if the "good agent" is just one who is better at convincing them to buy stuff they don't need?

Think of it this way: have you ever asked people for a referral for a salesperson? For example, when you bought your last car, did you ask around for someone who was really adept at selling cars? Of course not, because the last thing you want to do is have to negotiate with a wily salesperson.

That's why so few agents are able to build a dependable business solely from personal referrals. It's an incredibly uphill battle to fight the perception that the quality of the agent who helps you buy or sell a house makes a meaningful difference. Yes, some agents do build that type of following, but it takes a long time to build the kind of reputation that can overcome the common presumption that real estate agents are just salespeople.

The Original Sin

As Confucius said, "The beginning of wisdom is to call things by their proper name." Conversely, the beginning of foolishness is to call things by their improper name, and we've all been calling real estate agents by the wrong name for years. You remember the story of the original sin with Adam and Eve, happy and naked, frolicking around in the Garden of Eden without a care in the world. Then, unfortunately, they listened to that stupid snake, chose to take a bite out of that forbidden fruit, got kicked out, and relegated humankind to the nastiness of the outside world. The original sin triggered by eating that apple ruined everything, right from the beginning. Famine, war, disease—they all stem from that original sin.

This misconception that real estate agents are just salespeople is like that—like an original sin at the heart of our industry. It's a mistake that we made right at the beginning, like a construction flaw in the foundation of a building, and it's the source of almost all the major problems in the industry.

Words matter. Words are powerful. Words have consequences. What we call ourselves influences how people see us, how we see ourselves, and how we act. By calling real estate agents salespeople for a generation, the industry has cultivated a constricting sales-dominated mind-set that has had a devastating impact on us. It's prejudiced the way that the public sees us. It's undermined our ability to generate trusting relationships with our clients and our potential clients. It contributes toward both agent dissatisfaction and broker unprofitability. It's undercut the quality of the service we provide to buyers and sellers.

Ultimately, this mistaken label has made us vulnerable to the Disruptors, Discounters, and Doubters. And we only have ourselves to blame. We've been so focused on ourselves, and so focused on our short-term needs to generate a sale, that we've completely ignored the needs of our clients. We need to flip that mentality and start thinking about our clients, and not about ourselves.

So how do we change? The whole point of Client-Oriented Real Estate is to focus relentlessly on the needs of our clients. We need to think expansively about what they need and creatively about the ways in which we can satisfy those needs. Our me-centered focus on our own needs has left us uniquely vulnerable to both internal and external threats to our prevailing business model. Essentially, if we're not going to pay careful attention to what clients need from us, or find creative ways to address those needs, someone else will.

And that starts with getting better at our jobs.

Key #2: Be Great at Our Jobs

LET ME ASK YOU A SIMPLE QUESTION: *If you were no longer in the real estate business, but knowing everything you know, would you be willing to list your home with more than 50 percent of the agents in your market?*

Seriously, just think about it for a minute. You've worked in your local industry, so you probably have a good sense of your colleagues' abilities, since you've done deals with some of them, worked in the same office with others, and know many of the rest. If you left the business tomorrow, and had to then list your home, would you be willing to work with over half the agents you know?

I've asked that question of dozens of audiences of my colleagues over the last ten years, and the results are frightening.

Nobody raises their hands. Nobody.

Seriously. Nobody. It's embarrassing. I usually have to check to make sure the mic is working. Yup! Working fine! They can hear me all right. They're just not raising their hands.

So then I lower the bar and ask this: *Okay, well, would you be willing to work with at least 33 percent of the agents in your market?*

This time, I get a smattering of hands, but still not a lot. It's only when I drop down to 25 percent that I start to get a majority of my audience members agreeing. Time after time, the audiences I speak to would only work with about a quarter of the agents in their local industry.

And it's the same reaction across the country, regardless of whether I'm talking to a group of broker-owners, industry professionals, or agents themselves. Every time I ask the question, I find that most of the people in the industry wouldn't work with the vast majority of the agents in their area.

That's astonishing. I mean, would I get the same response if I asked other service professionals? What if I asked a room full of doctors? Would they be like, "Oh, no way, I'm not going to see ol' Doctor Widowmaker over there!"

But that's what I get from real estate professionals. And my guess is that you'd tell me the same thing, because you've had the experience of doing deals with agents in your area who are simply not good at their jobs, whom you had to carry throughout the entire transaction.

Yet, those agents are still in the business. They still sell homes. And they take deals away from the people like you who care about the quality of the work you do.

We shouldn't be surprised that we have this kind of service problem in the real estate industry. Indeed, we can't necessarily blame the agents themselves for this problem. It's not their fault. If we thought that 90 percent of the agents in the industry were proficient at their jobs, then we could certainly hold the remaining 10 percent accountable for their lack of commitment or ability. But when we ourselves acknowledge that over 75 percent of the agents working in the business are not particularly competent, then we have to recognize that this stems from a systemic failure in the industry itself.

After all, we don't hire for competence. We don't train for competence. We don't create systems to support competence. Why? Because the real estate industry sees real estate agents only as traditional salespeople whose only role is to generate leads and turn them into transactions. We hire for sales, train for sales, create systems for sales, and direct all our innovative energy toward sales. Why should we expect that most agents will be competent at their jobs of helping people buy and sell real estate when we've built the entire industry based on the mind-set that they're simply salespeople?

Think about how our industry is structured. We build brokerages around a sales-based, independent contractor model that encourages come-one-come-all hiring standards. We emphasize training systems that are exclusively designed to teach agents how to prospect for leads, without any real instruction on how to do the actual job of helping people buy or sell homes. We innovate wonderful new technologies that are specifically designed to generate leads and do nothing to help agents guide their clients through the complex transactional minefield.

That sales-dominant mind-set affects everyone in the industry, from the heads of franchise systems to the owners of big brokerages to the vendors to the trainers and coaches, all the way to the agents in the field. I can't tell you how many times I've been to a conference where a speaker fired up an audience of real estate agents by telling them that their job was not helping people buy and sell real estate, their only job was "to get out there and PROSPECT!"

Everyone always applauds. Lustily.

But that's crazy! That's not your only job. Yes, you need to generate clients for yourself, but what do you do next? If you don't know how to actually service that client's needs, you're like a dog chasing a car—the car stops, and the dog looks at it like, "Damn, what am I supposed to do now?"

Be Great at Your Job

You know what most top real estate agents have in common? They're almost always great at their jobs.

It's really that simple. Successful agents don't conform to the superficial stereotypes that we all have of the dynamic superstars out of central casting. They're not all magnetic, gregarious backslappers who overwhelm you with the persuasive force of their personality. Indeed, some of the most effective agents I know are quiet, modest, button-down technicians whom you would never dream would be successful in a sales business.

Just take a look at the people who win awards in your market for their production every year and see whether you can find any kind of common denominator. What you'll discover is that great real estate agents come in all shapes and sizes. Some are charming, others are boring. Some are loud, others are quiet. Some are likable, others are abrasive. Some are neat, others are sloppy. Some prospect like crazy, others never pick up the phone. Young, old, attractive, plain, short, tall, skinny, not skinny—they're all over the map.

But they almost all have one thing in common: they're almost always highly competent at the practice of real estate. They're smart at pricing homes, they're diligent at learning inventory, they're savvy at negotiating, they're wise at counseling clients, they're skilled at facilitating a transaction, and they work hard. That's why they are so successful, because being proficient at helping people buy and sell homes is the most important driver of a successful real estate business. If you're accurate at pricing listings, then you'll sell more of them. If you're empathetic in counseling buyers, you'll get more of them into contract. If you're clever at facilitating a transaction, you'll close more of them.

Most importantly, of course, if you're great at your job, your satisfied clients will work with you the next time they need to buy or sell a home, so you'll be able to generate a reliable repeat business. They'll tell their friends to use you, which will help you build a consistent flow of referral business. And they'll write stunning testimonials that will provide ironclad validation whenever you're trying to win over a new client.

On the other hand, you'll never be a top producer if you're, well, bad at your job. Your overpriced or poorly marketed listings will expire. Your neglected buyers who are tired of looking at the wrong homes will find another agent. Your ill-constructed deals will fall apart. You'll never get repeat business because no one will want to work with you again. And you'll certainly never receive referrals because why would someone recommend an agent who failed to find them a home or blew up their deal?

In the end, it doesn't matter if you're one of those people that everyone thinks is a natural-born salesman because of your effervescent personality. It doesn't matter how much you prospect with your memorized power scripts designed to trick sellers into listing with you. Eventually, you'll be out of the business.

So how do we get past that? How do we address the competency problem in the real estate industry?

It's actually quite simple: we need to be great at our jobs. Our actual jobs. The job of helping people buy and sell real estate.

Hiring

We need to start right from the beginning by changing the fog-the-mirror hiring standards generally employed by brokerages throughout the country. After all, most brokers are built on an independent contractor model, with a few management employees and a huge workforce of salespeople (there, I said the dreaded word) who do not get salaries or other benefits and who are compensated solely by commissions for deals they close.

With this model, brokers have little incentive to maintain exacting hiring standards, since they don't think it costs much to add new salespeople, and even the most inept and unpromising applicant might be able to sell a house or two to members of his or her immediate family. And since the barriers to entry for real estate are generally low—fewer than a hundred hours of licensing instruction, and a multiple-choice test—brokers often are choosing from an applicant pool that got into the industry because people think it's easy.

Even worse, I think that most brokers hire agents based on the wrong perceived skill set. Here's an example: You're at a restaurant, and the server is friendly and bubbly, and a broker will say, "Man, she'd make a great real estate agent!" As if the job of being a real estate agent is like being a greeter at Walmart. We should be interviewing agents about their ability to manage projects, to handle stress, to communicate, not just looking for superficial social skills.

So what should we do? Mostly, brokers need to be more exacting in their hiring standards, because they need to realize that unskilled agents actually cost them money. They take up space; they distract managers and trainers; and they take clients away from agents who might actually be able to service (and close) them. As brokers, we hire them because we figure they're not drawing a salary, and maybe they can at least sell their brothers and sisters and best friends a house next year. And then we keep them around because we look at our rosters and think, "Well, that guy might be a complete dolt, but he did sell three houses last year." I get it. It's tough to fire that guy, especially when low-producing agents like that are at relatively low splits and generate superficially profitable company dollars.

But what we often overlook is that those three sales probably came from company-generated leads that would have gone to better agents if they hadn't been misdirected to the schmo. Maybe we overlook how much manager time was spent trying to keep those deals together. And we overlook how that agent got five other company clients who might have bought or sold a house if they'd worked with one of our better agents. Perhaps we overlook how often bad agents create reputations that undermine the brand identity we spend so much time and money building up.

Again, I get it. It takes a leap of faith to fire agents who appear to be generating profits for the company, particularly when margins are so tight. But can we at least do a better job screening agents when we hire them in the first place? Can we look for people who have sound emotional intelligence, say, rather than superficial social skills?

If you want to think a little more aggressively, how about creating an apprenticeship system in the industry? What are we doing taking agents right off the street, fresh from their licensing exam, and inflicting them directly on clients? One of the promising aspects of modern agent teams is that the collaboration might lead to more apprentice-style development programs where new agents learn how to do the job, not just from education but from shadowing a more seasoned professional going through her day.

Education

Which brings us to the next competency issue: the way we educate agents. We hire these unskilled workers, and then we put them through an education and training industry that never actually teaches them how to do their jobs of helping people buy and sell homes.

Here's an example. Years ago, my company used to run an incubator system—a prospecting office where all the new agents would go to take classes in the morning, then do supervised lead-generation activities all afternoon. One day, after teaching a traditional cold-calling prospecting class, I watched while the agents made their calls for a few hours. About an hour into the session, one of the agents came up to me and said, "Hey, it worked!"

"What do you mean?" I asked.

"I called someone and they said they're thinking about moving!"

"Wow, great, so what'd you do?"

"Well, nothing yet. They're on hold."

Basically, this guy knew how to chase a car, but had no idea what to do when it stopped. That, in a nutshell, is the real estate industry's educational industry, which is dominated by the sales coaching programs that are entirely devoted to teaching prospecting.

Go to any convention or conference and you'll see class after class about how to prospect for business or close deals with your clients—whether through referral databases, farming, cold calling,

FSBOs, expireds, social media, personal marketing, or whatever. Every program has scripts and dialogues that will help you generate your next lead, or close your next client. Whatever the system, they all have one thing in common: they focus on how to generate leads, not about what you need to do once you get them. They're all about sales, not service. They all conceive of real estate agents as simply salespeople. And they're all about chasing the car.

Now, don't get me wrong. Many of those sales coaching programs are terrific. I have enormous respect for trainers like Tom Ferry, Brian Buffini, Larry Kendall, Verl Workman, and the many others who over the years have done amazing training to help agents build their businesses. Certainly, agents need to learn fundamental sales skills if they want to be successful.

But even if that kind of education is necessary, it's simply not sufficient for helping agents build their careers. Agents also need to learn what to do after they actually generate those clients. They need to learn the substantive skills that go into providing impeccable client-service experience: how to counsel clients, stage homes, qualify buyers, create marketing, present offers, negotiate deals, solve problems, and manage an infuriatingly complex transactional process. Where is the training that helps real estate agents actually become great at their jobs?

They're not learning how to do their job when they study for their licenses. Most licensing education is a dry recitation of archaic laws and regulations that are mostly designed to scare people into not breaking the law. No one ever comes out of a licensing class knowing the first thing about how to actually help a client buy or sell a home.

They're not learning how to do their job in their mandatory ethics training. Ethics are important, of course, but they're only a minimum baseline for establishing competency. Teaching an agent ethical practice is not the same skill as teaching her how to be good at her job. An agent passing an ethics class is like a restaurant passing an inspection: it's nice to know that they don't have too many mice in the kitchen, but that doesn't mean that the food is any good.

They're not learning how to do their job in their continuing education. Sadly, most agents look forward to continuing ed classes the way they look forward to a trip to the dentist: a necessary experience that they endure, rather than enjoy. Why? Because most of those classes are pasteurized pablum designed by committees to be as bland and inoffensive as possible. I know, I've taught it. And after years in the industry, I've learned that if I want to get a class approved for continuing education, all I have to do is water down all the interesting insights, sand off the sharp edges, and neuter anything that might actually be helpful to agents.

And agents aren't learning how to do their job when they get a certification or designation. A lot of these classes do teach some substantive skills and are certainly worthwhile. But many of them, too many of them, are really just money-making marketing gimmicks. You simply sit through a class where the instructor basically coaches you on how to pass the exam, and then get a certification that includes some initials after your name that you can use for marketing and networking—for as long as you continue to pay your annual fee for the privilege.

Too many of these courses are less about developing an agent's expertise than burnishing her credentials so that she can market that purported expertise—and be part of an overhyped referral network of other certified professionals. Like everything else about this industry, it's thinking like a salesperson, focusing on whether that accreditation will help us market ourselves, not whether it will teach us skills that we need.

Sadly, agents get the education industry they want and deserve. They want to learn how to generate leads, so the best educators like Ferry and Buffini go into sales coaching. Agents hate being forced to take mandatory education, so they simply try to make it as painless as possible. And the only way to lure them into skill development classes is to promise them a certification that will generate business, rather than making the more complicated argument that a proper certification program will actually help them become better at their jobs.

So we need to show agents the connection between skilled client service and professional success. We need to show them that being great at your actual job is the key to being successful at your actual job. If they're great at their job, their listings sell, their buyers buy, their transactions hold together, and they'll get paid. Even better, if they're great at their job, they'll slowly build the kind of referral business that's the foundation for almost all highly successful real estate careers.

Agents themselves have to do their part. They need to make a commitment to actually learning how to become great at their jobs. They can't take the easy way out by looking for the easiest continuing education classes that will satisfy their requirements, or the certifications that will generate the most business. If they're going to get sales coaching, they should combine that with education that will teach them what to do when they "catch the car."

Ultimately, though, we have to give them better options. If we want an industry where we can trust way more than 25 percent of the real estate agents, we need to build a more ambitious educational infrastructure. We need licensing education that does more than teach regulatory compliance, continuing ed that treats ethics as a baseline rather than a goal, and certifications that have more rigorous application standards and ongoing compliance requirements.

Essentially, we need to put the same kind of creative energy into substantive skills training that we put into sales coaching. Education should be interesting, and the most engaging training in the industry comes from those sales coaches. Why? Because they have a point of view, an edge, a perspective. Tom Ferry has that. Brian Buffini has that. Lots of national trainers have that, because they have to grab and keep your attention if they want to earn your money. They're willing to take chances.

But if you get training from an individual broker, or your board, or a franchise system, or NAR, you tend to get something produced by a committee that did its best to hone off any of the interesting sharp edges, blur the point of view, provide a generic perspective, and be all things to all people. That's not interesting.

Education should be dynamic. It should be daring. It should take the chance of offending you, of challenging you, of spurring disagreement and debate. I don't always agree with Tom or Brian when I hear them, but they make me think. They make me better. But if I go to some approved-by-committee training program, I don't disagree with anything. Why? Because it's all inoffensive, well-intentioned, tried-and-true, smoothed-over, bullet-pointed conventional wisdom.

The bottom line is this: if we think that only a quarter of the agents in the field are good at their jobs, we need to do a better job educating them.

Systems and Standards

If we want agents to deliver better service experiences for their clients, we also need to give them tools, systems, and programs that can help them do great work—and make their jobs easier. We give agents an abundance of tools to help them do lead generation, and then almost nothing to guide them through the transactional process.

In other industries, business owners can ensure high levels of quality service by creating mandatory systems and standards. They might, for example, have an operations manual that spells out in granular detail how employees need to do their jobs. Let's say you work at Starbucks. You make a frappuccino the way they tell you to make a frappuccino. You work at a law firm, you file a case and write your briefs according to the standards set by the partnership.

Indeed, I've always found it odd that real estate franchises have evolved more as brand franchises than format franchises. In most cases, you sign on with a big real estate franchise, and you'll get access to tools and resources, but rarely do you get the kind of blueprint for running a successful operation that you'd get from a format franchise in retail or food service. When you get a franchise with McDonald's, you don't get to decide how you're going to make the burgers. You make the burgers the way McDonald's tells you to make the burgers, based on best practices that have developed over years of trial and error.

Basically, in most businesses, you get systems that guide you about how to do your job. But we don't do that in real estate. Part of the reason is the independent contractor model, which legally restricts brokers from *mandating* how agents perform their work. So as a broker, I'm not supposed to be able to tell my agents how I want them to show a home, or negotiate a deal, or manage a transaction. And that's incredibly frustrating.

My company provides our agents with incredible support systems to help them do their jobs better, but we can't make anyone use them. No matter how competent we are as a brokerage, we're at the mercy of that last link in the chain—the agent sitting with that client, to actually implement the tools we give her. Unlike the owner of a hotel, or the manager of a restaurant, I can't oversee what the agent is doing and help her along the way to make the right decisions. I'm not at that kitchen table presenting the value package. I'm not in the car going to a showing.

That makes it almost impossible, as a brokerage, to ensure consistent, quality service. A client could walk into one of my offices today, get an agent, and have a happy experience. Another client could walk into that same office, get a different agent, and be miserable throughout the whole process. Same company, same systems, same tools—but two different agents, so two different experiences.

We need to change that, from the top down starting with franchise brands, then big brokers, then everyone in the industry. We need to identify best practices for servicing our buyers and sellers, incorporate those best practices into a standard program, and then codify them into policies and procedure manuals, checklists, project plans, or whatever else will guide agents about how to do their job well. We know what it takes to do outstanding work for our clients. Why don't we work harder to ensure that every agent raises the bar on their own performance?

Brokers especially need to get over this risk-averse, namby-pamby fear of running afoul of independent contractor laws. Yes, that's always a risk, but brokers are already routinely violating independent contractor laws in a variety of other ways: mandating affiliate business support, or prospecting methodologies, or technology adoption. In other words, they're already putting themselves at this kind of risk—they're just taking those risks for sales over service.

Indeed, what they should be doing is ensuring compliance with independent contractor laws in the other parts of their business, while still working to raise the bar on client service. If anything, the risk of setting standards and protocols for governing client care is much lower than what brokers are already doing to support their sales efforts. After all, in most states, brokers have a responsibility to supervise agents to ensure compliance with laws and regulations.

In that kind of regulatory environments, brokers are certainly allowed to establish fundamental service standards to protect the clients by ensuring that they get a better service experience. Indeed, I would argue that consumer protections don't just *allow* brokers to set standards, they *require* brokers to set standards! (All that said, I should clarify that although I'm a lawyer, I'm not *your* lawyer, and you should talk to a lawyer if you have concerns about maintaining the independent contractor status of your agents.)

This kind of support is exactly what agents need to provide a higher level of client service. I understand that some would bristle at the idea of the broker "telling me what to do," but in most cases agents would welcome systems and standards that would allow them to do their jobs more efficiently and effectively without having to constantly figure things out for themselves. But an industry leery of violating independent contractor standards gives agents surprisingly little technical or logistical support for servicing their clients' needs. We need to change that.

Direct Services

Being a real estate agent is hard work. As we've discussed, agents really have two jobs, because they have to take on both the sales and service roles. So why don't we try to find ways to make their jobs easier?

One of the easiest ways we could improve client service in the real estate industry would be to provide more direct, automated services directly from the broker (or franchise) to the client. In other words, instead of relying on agents to do all the work, we find ways to do some of the work for them.

I mean, isn't it a little strange that most clients have virtually no direct experience with their brokers? We're supposed to be supervising our agents' work, yet we often don't even know the names of the clients they're working with. We know the listed sellers, since they generally need to be submitted to our MLS systems, but we generally find out the names of the buyers only when they, you know, go into contract. That's a little crazy.

Now, I know that some agents will bristle at the idea of their broker maintaining any tangible relationship to their clients. But I'm not talking about supplanting the agent-client relationship; I'm talking about supplementing it by taking some of the burden off the agent's shoulders.

For example, my company went on an initiative several years ago to try to create systems that would support agents by automating communication updates directly from the broker. Every week, sellers got a series of emails that came from the company, but looked as if they came from the agent. One was an update about what was happening in their local market, to help sellers stay on top of what their competition was doing: new listings, price changes, status changes, and vital information like that. Another was a weekly property traffic update, so that sellers could see how well the online marketing was going.

The point of the emails was to ensure a steady line of communication between the agent and the client, without actually requiring the agent to do anything. These types of communication made the agent's job easier, if only by reducing the number of update calls that the client made to find out what was happening with the market or the marketing.

Introducing these kinds of services isn't easy, particularly in an era of declining broker margins. But we've found that systems that make agents' jobs easier are a sound investment, since they often become ideal retention tools.

Managerial Responsibilities

As brokers, we expect too much out of our managers, our office leaders. Think about the different types of responsibilities we generally give them:

- *Office Administration.* They usually have to manage an office facility, which means everything from hiring employees to procuring supplies to managing a budget.

- *Coaching.* We ask them to be agent coaches, guiding them in formulating and following business plans.

- *Training.* They need to be able to run office meetings and in-office training programs.

- *Recruiting.* They're generally required to recruit agents to their offices, both newly licensed agents and seasoned professionals.

- *Deal Doctoring.* We expect them to be experts at helping their agents keep difficult deals together.

- *Cultural Ambassador.* Managers are the company representative in fostering the company culture within the office.

- *Affiliate Conversion.* We often expect them to do all this while they promote our affiliate home services businesses.

Those are a lot of hats to wear. Even worse, those are a lot of different types of jobs that require a diverse skill set. They need the organizational skills to administer the office and handle deal problems, the sales skills to drive recruiting and affiliate adoption, and the communication skills to be an effective coach and trainer. It's not easy finding someone who excels at all those roles. Indeed, if you find someone who skillfully handles all the aspects of real estate office management, they're probably a risk to run off and start their own company.

Most likely, we all have managers who are highly competent at some aspects of the job and weak at others. The question becomes, then, where do we make the compromises—that is, what roles do we prioritize in managerial hiring and training?

Let's put it this way: If you're an owner or broker, how would you rank the seven management roles I just outlined? What would be first? In my experience, and I've asked lots of brokers about this, the most popular choice as the most important managerial role is recruiting, and second is affiliate conversion. Why? Because most brokers, like most agents, think like salespeople. That is, they're most likely to prioritize what they perceive as revenue-generating activities such as recruiting and conversion, rather than softer responsibilities in coaching, training, culture, or deal doctoring.

I can understand why: recruiting and conversion are easy to measure. A manager who recruits a lot of agents makes a dramatically visible impact to the office. You can see it in the monthly numbers, a bunch of new names on the roster. The same with affiliate adoption—you usually get a number every month that's a straight percentage of opportunities and conversion.

You can't measure the impact of the other managerial roles as easily. How do you monetize the strength of an office culture? How do you calculate the sense of well-being in an office that is simply well run and well maintained? How do you track the value of well-placed advice on putting a deal together?

Yes, you can get a rough measure of a manager's coaching and managerial abilities by maybe tracking agent production each year, but those numbers can be impacted by market conditions, general volatility, and other factors. It's tough to get as much of a bright-line measure as you can get, say, with recruiting, where you add every dollar.

All of this is to say that we often emphasize the recruiting and conversion responsibilities with our managers the same way that we stress lead generation with our agents. We recruit managers based on their perceived ability to recruit and reward them for their recruiting success, when the best managers are often those that are better at nurturing their agents in immeasurable but vital ways. And that emphasis has an impact on agent competence and on the quality of the experience they give their clients.

So how can we address this? For one thing, we could do a better job of training our managers in all the responsibilities we're going to put on them. Too many brokers (including, at times, me) simply hire an experienced agent, slap a managerial badge on them, and figure she knows how to manage. But you don't necessarily learn how to manage real estate agents by being one. Even when we do have managerial training programs, they mostly spend all their time on recruiting, with almost no attention to the roles that help support agent performance. They're all about teaching managers to chase the car.

Moreover, more brokers should consider separating out managerial roles. Some brokers I know, for example, have abandoned the idea of having a manager on-site in every office and, instead, have centralized managers working out of a corporate location who have distinct roles: one is recruiting, another is the company deal doctor, another runs coaching, and so on. Not only does this allow for specialization of roles, but it can also eliminate costs by reducing the number of managers you need per office.

However we do it, we absolutely need to enlist managers in the drive to increase agent competency and improve client-service experiences.

Finally, we need to make great client service part of our industry culture. Because the real estate industry has been conceived of solely as a sales industry, we've built a cultural mind-set that glorifies sales abilities and pays almost no attention to service skills. We all need to do more to create a culture that celebrates and validates client service:

- *Client Ratings*. Embrace meaningful client ratings through third-party validation companies like RealSatisfied to create agent accountability, send a message to clients that their opinions matter, and monitor client satisfaction.

- *Agent Ratings*. You want to do something really revolutionary? Have agents rate their experiences doing deals with other agents, and publish that at least within the professional community. We could use more peer review in this industry.

- *Awards*. Give agents awards not just for production, but for heartfelt reviews that demonstrate a true commitment to client service.

- *Rewards*. Create commission plans that bump splits, waive fees, or create bonuses that reward superior client satisfaction.

Everyone responds to incentives, so why don't we create the kind of incentives that will drive a more consistent quality client-service experience? Most importantly, we need to use this commitment to client service as more than just another marketing tool. If we have high client-satisfaction ratings that we can use in our listing presentations, that's terrific. But that's not why we should be measuring client service. We need to know whether our clients are having a satisfactory or excellent experience so that we can learn what works, and what doesn't.

For example, do you ever wonder why so many agents have nothing but five-star satisfaction reviews? Well, for one reason, it's because of a selection bias that develops when most reviews are agent-initiated—the agent pesters her happy clients to write reviews and maybe is somewhat less enthusiastic about following up with her unhappy clients. Moreover, most people are generally nice, and they don't like to say bad things about an agent they might have worked with for many months. It just seems mean, and, even worse, they don't want to get an angry phone call from an agent they criticized in a review.

But the biggest reason most agents get decent reviews is that we generally only survey people who completed their transactions, which tends to influence the ratings in two ways. First, people who close their deals are generally relieved it's all over, so they're in a happier frame of mind than they were during the term of the transaction. Second, and more important, we get a skewed sample if we only survey the people who successfully bought or sold a home with us.

What if we surveyed all the people who stopped working with us because we didn't answer their initial email inquiry in time, or weren't available when they called for appointments, or just weren't happy with the quality of our service? If we want a true measure of client satisfaction, we should be surveying those people as well. But we don't, because our commitment to client reviews is often just an attempt to get a good talking point about "excellent client satisfaction" for our listing presentations.

We also need to start measuring metrics other than sales production. What percentage of an agent's listings actually sell within their initial term? What's her average listing price retention rate? How long are her listings on the market? How do these figures compare to the average agent in the area? These are all indicators of performance and are easily calculable from any MLS system, but we don't spend enough time looking at them or using them to help agents become better at their jobs.

Again, the first instinct many industry people have with regard to performance indicators is to find a way to use them to market agents to consumers—in other words, focusing entirely on generating sales rather than on improving service. But performance indicators are excellent coaching tools if we want to help agents identify and adhere to best practices.

Similarly, agents should be doing more on their own to ensure that their clients have a remarkable service experience. They should seek out brokerages that are committed to providing a quality full-service experience for clients, and which will provide them with the systems they need to take care of their clients. And on an individual basis, they should be setting their own standards, creating their own systems, and making their own commitment to raising the bar on the industry. Agent by agent, broker by broker, we can change the industry's approach to client service and satisfaction.

What Do We Know Now?

In short, here's the client-oriented approach for improving the client-service experience in our industry: Hire agents who have the ability to do exemplary work. Educate them about how to do the job of helping people buy and sell homes. Give them the support and services to help them service their clients' needs, in both company systems and managerial leadership. And then build a culture that emphasizes and rewards excellence in client service.

Once we've created the kind of industry that helps agents become highly proficient at their jobs, we have to give them something great to offer. We need to modernize the value proposition we provide to our clients—our next key to change.

Key #3: Modernize Our Value Proposition: The CORE Services

"ALL REAL ESTATE AGENTS ARE THE SAME."
How many times have you heard that? It's really frustrating and particularly galling to agents who work hard for their clients, who try to provide a superb service experience, and who actually make a professional living. You know we're not all the same. You know that a great agent can make a difference for a client.

So why don't the clients know that? The sad truth about the real estate industry is that people aren't choosy enough about who helps them buy or sell a house. They'll walk into real estate offices and take the "up person." They'll click on the "find out more" button on the website and take whoever shoots them a quick email. They'll pop into an open house and take the nice agent who's hosting. They'll turn to their friend from the club, even though she's a part-timer who hasn't sold a house in years. Simply put, they're not demanding enough about whom they hire to help them buy or sell a home.

Indeed, the real estate industry doesn't try to fight this mentality—we embrace it! We've built extensive lead-generation methodologies based on the premise that leads are not choosy. That's why we have uptime, and do open houses, and build flashy websites. It's why brokers will hire pretty much anyone, since even the ghastliest real estate agent probably has at least one second cousin who will still hire him to sell her house.

Yes, some of this is changing. Publicly published agent ratings and reviews, for example, have become much more common in the past few years, providing a way for clients to vet potential agents. I expect we'll start seeing more websites that provide performance metrics to evaluate agents based on the percentage of listings taken that sell, days-on-market, listing retention rates, and measures like that.

But we're still a long way from an industry where clients routinely demand to work with the best agents. All you have to do is look at a production report from your local MLS and see how many hapless agents are still managing to sell four or five houses a year, and how many mediocre brokers are doing enough business to at least keep the lights on. And that all adds up.

In most of my markets, at least half the deals are closed each year by a large mass of agents who sell fewer than five homes a year—and who each make less than the receptionists who answer their phones. If more clients were demanding, then those agents, and those brokers, would be out of business. But they're not. So they're not.

So why aren't clients more demanding when they hire a real estate agent? It starts with the original sin I discussed earlier—the misconception that real estate agents are salespeople. Essentially, people are simply not that choosy when they hire a salesperson because, from a consumer's perspective, all salespeople really are the same.

Remember the last time you were buying a car? You probably researched all the brands in your price range, read the consumer reviews, and asked your friends about their own experiences. But did you think about who was going to sell you the car? Did that make a difference to you? No, because we don't make purchasing decisions based on the salesperson—a salesperson is a salesperson is a salesperson.

They're all the same—all the salespeople, all the brokers, even all the real estate brands. This commodification extends all the way to the top. The most popular real estate brands in the country—Century 21, Coldwell Banker, Weichert, ERA, Keller Williams, RE/MAX—are well-associated with the general concept of real estate, but they say little about the kind of real estate services they provide. To the public, they're all basically the same, like gas stations and convenience stores.

Put it this way: can you think of any specific association that the average consumer would have with any of those brands? Maybe people would still remember Century 21's gold jackets, which have been retired for years, but that's about it. Indeed, the only "flavor" that most real estate brands develop comes from their connection outside of real estate: Sotheby's International Realty has a high-end association because of its relationship to the auction house; Better Homes and Gardens Real Estate has a home-and-hearth appeal because of the iconic brand of the magazine; and Berkshire Hathaway HomeServices carries a certain financial services brand angle because of its connection to investor Warren Buffett. But those associations only developed because franchises piggybacked on established, iconic brands, not because of anything the franchises themselves did.

For the most part, real estate brands have become commodified, which says little about the kinds of services that they give to clients. There's no Apple of real estate, no Nordstrom, no Four Seasons. They're all the same.

This kind of environment—an all-agents-are-the-same com-modification—is the perfect breeding ground for Discounters. This is exactly what they want, to blur the lines between professional real estate providers and stripped-down impersonators. After all, if people think that all agents are the same, why pay more for the same service?

So now we have hundreds of Discounters across the internet, charging flat fees or offering a menu of services to sellers and making commission rebates back to buyers, all capitalizing on this corrosive public perception. (And I'm not even counting the traditional agents who will cut their fees at the first sign of an objection—we'll deal with these Doubters later.)

We've had Discounters for years, of course, and they've never taken more than a small share of the market. But they're a bigger threat than they've ever been before—not because of anything they've done, but because of what we as an industry *haven't* done.

Specifically, we haven't adapted. We haven't adjusted our value proposition for buyers or sellers to account for the technological advances over the last twenty-five years. We're still making the kinds of presentations and pitching the same set of services that we were a generation ago, even as the business has become more challenging and the real estate transaction more complex.

Think back to the 1990s. Before real estate went on the internet, we had enormous advantages over the Discounters, relegating them to a small, sad corner of the industry—the land of bargain hunters and low-ballers. And our value propositions for both sellers and buyers reflected that domination. For sellers, we provided exclusive access to a network of brokers, agents, and buyers, and marketed homes through expensive newsprint advertising (and later, portal syndication) that was difficult for low-revenue Discounters to match. And for buyers, we were the literal gatekeeper of information, with the keys to opening the door to the inventory of homes that were for sale.

But times have changed, and we haven't changed with them.

Modernizing the Seller Value Proposition

Let's start with the value proposition for sellers. Traditionally, it was simple: we will market your listings to the largest possible audience of brokers, agents, and buyers. Sellers needed us to get into MLS, and they valued the kind of newsprint advertising that was difficult to provide by brokers on a discounted commission. So we created real differentiation between full-service brokers and the Discounters who couldn't match our MLS network and our costly marketing distributional breadth.

That differentiation in our seller value proposition continued even as the internet brought all those listings online, rendering newsprint obsolete. Full-service brokers and agents still had an advantage over the Discounters because internet marketing was complex and expensive. Even as third-party portals like Zillow and Trulia developed, brokers needed a certain amount of technical sophistication to enable listing syndication. Discounters couldn't quite keep up, so brokers were able to build a value proposition around their wide distribution of listings.

Ultimately, every full-service broker listing presentation in the country had a slide or a page with dozens of real estate website logos on it, trumpeting how they would market your home all over the internet. My company even trademarked the phrase, "Your Buyer Could Be Anywhere, So We're Everywhere."

But so-called listing syndication is not really a differentiator anymore, is it? Why? Because *everyone* is everywhere. Virtually every broker, large or small, full-service or Discounter, can plaster a home listing on hundreds of real estate sites. They can do it for free, and they can usually do it without any technical knowledge whatsoever. They just need to submit that listing to their MLS system, opt in to syndication, and they're everywhere.

Unfortunately, the average agent still talks about the services she provides as if it's 2005. Take, the typical listing presentation, when an agent goes into some seller's living room and makes a pitch that basically lays out these ten claims:

1. "My company is great!"

2. "I'm great too!"

3. "I'm going to market your home to the entire MLS."

4. "I'm going to market your home with beautiful photos."

5. "I'm going to market your home through beautiful marketing materials."

6. "I'm going to market your home on our great website."

7. "I'm going to market your home all over the internet."

8. "I'm going to market your home with open houses."

9. "I'm going to market your home through direct mail."

10. "I'm going to give you great service!"

Now, you might quibble with some of the particulars here, maybe you do things a little differently at your company. But I've worked with thousands of agents over the years, and I've seen their listing presentations. More or less, that's what they say.

And that's an absolutely abysmal value proposition for real estate agents today. Why? Because it's all about marketing, particularly the type of distributional marketing that can be easily and cheaply replicated by a Discounter.

Just look at most of those ten claims: pictures, materials, website, Zillow and other portals, open houses, direct mail. Agents talk about themselves and their company, pay lip service to giving "great service," and the rest is all about marketing. Indeed, most of them call this the marketing presentation, since that's all they talk about—and all they think they have to offer.

Even worse, this traditional value proposition makes us uniquely vulnerable to Discounters who can easily and cheaply replicate most of those marketing services:

- They can hire a local photographer to take pictures, or even ask sellers to take the pictures themselves.

- They hire some kid in India for $1/hour to write flowery ad copy for the listings and to upload the listing data.

- They can get that listing into MLS just by becoming a member, paying their dues, and putting the listing out with a minimal offer of compensation.

- They can get that listing onto their own website (and your website!) just by submitting through IDX.

- They can get that listing on Zillow, Trulia, Realtor.com, and every other portal just by, in most cases, putting it in MLS.

- If the seller is willing to pay for it, they can send out a direct mail campaign with a couple of clicks on any number of websites.

- They can hire a local agent to do an open house or, again, enlist the sellers to do it themselves.

So they can just about duplicate the entire traditional marketing campaign for a few hundred dollars. They charge $500, pay out half that for their expenses for the photographer and the kid from India, and they make a 50 percent margin. They don't make a lot on each listing, but they can make it up in volume.

When people say that all brokers and agents are the same, that's what they're talking about: we all say the same things, and we all do the same things. So why pay a big commission when a Discounter can do the same thing for a few hundred dollars?

The most frustrating part of this whole problem is that marketing is one of the least important things we do for sellers. If we're going to differentiate ourselves, we need to start emphasizing and defining ourselves by all the other services we provide—in particular, the services that are not so easily and cheaply replicable.

So what are those services? I've been doing this exercise with agents for a long time, asking them to list all the services they do for their seller clients, and then taking all those tasks and organizing them into a suite of services that all great agents provide to sellers. Here they are:

1. *Consultation.* Great agents consult with the client about their needs: why they're moving, when they need to be out, what they're looking for in an agent and a company.

2. *Pricing.* Great agents review and explain the market environment, go over comps and competing listings, and guide the client through the process of setting the initial price of the home.

3. *Staging.* Great agents help the client clean, declutter, depersonalize, and ultimately even stage the property for maximum impact on buyers.

4. *Marketing.* Great agents provide a comprehensive marketing program that distributes the listing to the widest possible audience as well as target specific buyer demographics.

5. *Negotiation.* Great agents field all the offers, review them with the client, and advise them on how to negotiate the best terms of their sale.

6. *Transaction Management.* Great agents manage that deal through the transactional process (contract, inspections, mortgage, title, walkthrough) all the way to the closing, keeping everything on track and solving problems along the way.

7. *Communication.* And throughout that whole process, great agents provide a surpassing service experience by maintaining transparent communication and constantly updating the clients on what is happening with their sale.

(Yes, I understand that not all agents do all these tasks. But they should. That's why I say that great agents provide all these services. Because they actually do. That's why they're so successful at their jobs.)

I call these the seven CORE services, not only because they're client-oriented (thus the acronym CORE) but because they're crucial (through and through, to the core) to providing a great service experience to our clients. The CORE services take a client from that initial appointment all the way through to closing and highlight what agents actually need to do to service their clients' needs.

Now, marketing is obviously an important part of the service package, both because clients expect it and because marketing does indeed help sell homes. So it's right up there with the rest of the services agents provide to clients.

But it's not the only service that we do for sellers. And by over-emphasizing this basic laundry list of marketing tools in our value presentation, to the virtual exclusion of everything else, we've made ourselves particularly vulnerable to Discounters.

So we need to change the way we articulate our value proposition. We need to start talking more about services like consultation, staging, pricing, and transaction management. And we also need to start talking differently about traditional services, particularly in the way we explain the marketing we do.

Indeed, let's go through each of the seven CORE services and show how we should be articulating them for our clients to substantiate a contemporary—and differentiating—value package.

1. Turn Presentations into Consultations.

Let's start right from the beginning—that first meeting with our clients. The traditional listing presentation is a perfect example of the industry-centric model of real estate, because it's all about the agent: "Let me tell you about me and my company and my awards and my production and my experience and my ratings and my reference letters and, most of all, my twenty-seven-point marketing plan to get you what you want in the time you want—won't that be great!"

It's not the agents' fault. We've taught them wrong. It's all the original sin—we've taught agents to make presentations as if they're traveling salesmen selling vacuum cleaners door-to-door, rather than providing their clients with the kind of consultation that virtually every other service professional provides.

If I see a doctor, she starts with, "What hurts?" If I see a lawyer, he starts with, "What's your problem?" If I see a financial planner, a plumber, a hair stylist, an interior decorator, or really anyone who provides professional services, the first thing they do is ask me questions about myself. Why? For one thing, that's the best way to find out what the client needs and how to best provide it to them. But even more importantly, asking people questions about themselves, and showing an authentic interest in their answers, is the very best way to build rapport and trust with a client.

That's what we need to do in real estate. We need to stop thinking like salespeople and start thinking like service professionals. We've always taught the listing presentation as a sales opportunity, as a pitch to try to convince the seller to list with us. We have to flip that mind-set, to think of that listing appointment as the first chance we have to start servicing our clients' needs: to find out what their home is really worth, to learn what they need to do to get their home ready for the market, to calm their concerns about the process, to prepare them for what's ahead, and to inform them of the services we're going to provide them.

2. Redefine Pricing as a Crucial Service.

If we are to be completely honest with ourselves, the single most important service we provide to sellers is guiding them to price their home according to the prevailing market conditions. The marketing, the staging, and everything else we do is secondary. Simply put, if we do a good job in helping them price the home, it's probably going to sell. And if we don't, it's probably going to sit.

The funny thing is that we don't usually present pricing as a service we provide to sellers. That is, we provide a comparative market analysis on every presentation, but we rarely highlight strong pricing skills as a competitive advantage to a seller, even though our pricing guidance might be the most important thing we do.

Why don't we stress pricing as a service? For one thing, it's because we know that's not what the seller wants to hear. She doesn't want us to tell her how the best thing we can do for her is get her to face the realities of the market. The seller wants to hear how our marketing and staging are going to help get her *more* than the market. Even worse, we usually have to provide our pricing analysis before the seller has listed with us, which puts a lot of pressure on us to tell the client what she wants to hear if we want to walk out with that listing.

So how should we frame pricing? As a client-oriented collaborative process. In the traditional listing presentation, we taught agents to present pricing in a typically agent-centric way: "I'm the expert, trust me, this is where we should price the home." But because of the original sin, too many sellers don't really trust their agents (they perceive them as salespeople) about pricing—they think we're just trying to price the home for a quick sale. Moreover, pronouncing the price like that requires the agent to take ownership of the price, putting the agent on the defensive in cases where the seller thinks it's too low, and almost creating a negotiation between agent and client.

Why make pricing all about the agent? Instead, agents should present pricing from a client-oriented perspective: help educate the client about the market, guide them through the pricing process, and work collaboratively to identify the best market price. Instead of saying, "I'm the expert, here's the price," say, "Given what the market is telling us, where do you think we should price our listing?" Don't just pronounce the price; let the client discover it for herself. That invests the client in the decision-making process and takes the burden of defending the market off the agent.

In other words, the service we provide is not pricing the home. It's helping the seller price the home. Even more importantly, we should make clear to clients that this service continues throughout the marketing process, as we will help them track the changes in the market, and the feedback from agents and buyers, in adjusting the price point. Pricing is one of the most important services we provide—we should act like it is.

3. Elevate Staging as a Primary Service.

I'm shocked that so many agents still think of staging as an extra service provided only to fine homes by outside consultants, not something that's part of their core value proposition. In today's market, one of the most important services a great real estate agent can provide is helping the client prepare the home through decluttering, cleaning, depersonalizing, and everything else that goes into staging.

So why do so few agents emphasize their staging services for their clients? Partly it's because agents shy away from the awkward conversation of explaining to the sellers that they, you know, live like pigs. And too many agents aren't well trained on staging fundamentals, so they're insecure about their abilities and shirk off the responsibility to professional stagers. Because the concept of staging originated in the high-end homes, we still tend to associate it exclusively with luxury homes.

But that's all nonsense. Any home on the market can benefit from basic cleaning and decluttering, regardless of its price point. And virtually any agent can master the fundamentals of effective home presentation, learn how to communicate its value to her clients, and make staging a core part of her value proposition.

Most importantly, though, an agent who can provide staging services can really differentiate herself in the market. Since most agents delegate staging to experts, or charge extra for it, or provide it only for their high-end clients, agents who develop the expertise can certainly argue that they are "not the same." Certainly, staging skills can differentiate an agent from a Discounter, who cannot possibly provide an expert consultation about home preparation without expensive in-home visits by experts. You can't stage a home from Skype.

4. Find New Ways to Differentiate Marketing.

We talk about marketing all wrong. We're still highlighting distribution, as if it's 2005 and we can still impress a seller by showing her a list of the hundreds of useless websites that we're syndicating our listings to. And we also overemphasize marketing as our most important service for getting a home sold, even though it's certainly not as important as staging or pricing.

So how should we be talking about marketing? First, we need to stop emphasizing the size of our distribution and start focusing on how we can narrowly target our marketing to the perfect buyer pool. This kind of targeted advertising is much more viable than it was even five years ago, but we're still mostly doing generic online marketing to vast audiences of uninterested people.

Instead, we need to get beyond the bland and obvious "this house is inexpensive, so it will appeal to a new home buyer" and other types of banal recommendations to sellers. For example, we're already seeing start-ups like RealScout provide "big data" buyer intelligence to help agents identify prospective buyers before they even take a listing—an impressive tool to show sellers how they're different.

Second, we also need to commit to creating better content. Agents still take their own pictures without getting formal training in photography. They still write spotty and incomplete listing descriptions, with classic abbreviations like EIK and Ba/Br as if they're still putting together a classified ad where every character counts. Many still haven't made floor plans, 3-D walkthroughs, videos, or other effective visual marketing tools a part of their standard marketing program. Essentially, we're still doing the same mediocre marketing we were doing years ago, and the Discounters have caught up. Our marketing should be beautiful. It's not.

We need to get better. Agents need to either learn photography skills or commit to paying professional photographers for every listing. They need to start writing descriptions that tell an engaging story about the home, rather than just recite a boring litany of home features that are already detailed in the basic listing data. And they need to start using visual marketing tools like 3-D walkthroughs, floor plans, and video to separate themselves from Discounters and other agents.

Here's the best way to think about the kind of commitment we need to better marketing: we should all be taking whatever program we currently reserve for our luxury marketing and apply it to every listing we take. Yes, that requires spending more money, but if we invest a little more in our marketing programs, we can create separation from the Discounters—the same way that we used to separate ourselves through aggressive (and expensive) newspaper advertising.

5. Highlight the Impact of Negotiating Skills.

Great real estate agents absolutely need to be savvy negotiators—a crucial skill for getting sellers the best possible price for their home. Now, it's not as if we can sell a $400,000 home for $500,000 by sheer force of our immense persuasive powers. We're not Jedis. But we can make a difference on those margins—advising our sellers on how to get $5,000 more or our buyers on how to pay $5,000 less with clever negotiating.

The challenge with making negotiation part of our CORE value proposition is that almost all our clients think they're great negotiators. It's like driving, or lovemaking—everyone thinks that they're well above average. So you'll often be sitting across from a seller or buyer talking about the services you provide, and they'll pooh-pooh your negotiating ability—"Oh, we don't need that. I negotiate every day as part of my job!" These kinds of sellers, who don't see the need for professional negotiating services, are at risk of hiring a Discounter who requires the client do it herself, since they feel they're more than capable.

So how do we show that our negotiating skills provide real value to our clients? Even if we can't convince the seller we're a better negotiator, we still might be able to appeal to the value of using intermediaries: "Well, anyone with your experience in negotiation understands how helpful it can be to negotiate through an intermediary like me, so that you can stay above it all." It's a rhetorical gambit, but it has the advantage of actually being true.

More importantly, agents and brokers need to find metrics that quantify how professional negotiating can make a difference for the results their clients get. What's the average listing retention rate off your listings? What's your average listing discount that you get for your buyers? In individual cases, we don't really have control over the purchase price of the homes in our deals because so many variables can come into play. But over time, as those transactions build and we get a decent sample size, those metrics should demonstrate whether our negotiating skills are getting results for our clients. And if they do, we should make that a big part of our value proposition.

6. Emphasize the Complexity of Transaction Management.

Maybe the most underrated service that an agent provides her clients is to manage their transaction from that accepted offer through to closing. The very best agents are "deal doctors" who know how to keep a transaction together through all the trials and tribulations: handling inspection issues, facilitating a contract, overcoming title problems, smoothing mortgage complications, resolving walk-through disputes, and getting that seller to the closing table. After all, even if you're a wiz at pricing, conditioning, and marketing, you're not going to do a great job for your clients if all your deals fall apart.

So why don't more agents emphasize the importance of transaction management in their value proposition? For one thing, it's just not sexy. It's so much easier to show off our marketing, for example, because we have such pretty collateral: pictures, flyers, videos, mailings, all that good stuff. But transaction management is all about getting your hands dirty in the details, and it doesn't lend itself well to visuals. Also, agents may not want to emphasize how complicated and frustrating the transaction might be, because they might scare off a timid client.

Indeed, agents might also shy away from talking about transaction management because, like pricing, it often involves a certain amount of tough love—telling clients what they don't want to hear. After all, good transaction management skills often means talking stressed-out clients out of blowing up their own deal, which is a difficult talking point at a presentation: "Another valuable service I provide is keeping you from doing something really stupid! Isn't that wonderful? Shouldn't you definitely totally hire me?"

We need to get over this reluctance to talk about the gritty work we do keeping our transactions together. Why? Because effective transaction management is a service that Discounters cannot possibly match. Transaction management is time-intensive labor that requires local expertise and personal contacts with all the people involved with getting a client to closing. You can't do that from a call center in Bangladesh.

Indeed, transaction management might be the single best way to differentiate yourself from Discounters. They can argue that they provide the same marketing that we do, and they might claim they can price a home well through a simple automated value model (AVM), but they don't do anything meaningful to manage their clients through the transaction.

In a sense, we need to turn the frustrations of the transactional process to our advantage. If people perceive that buying or selling a home is hard, they're more likely to turn to professionals who have the expertise to make it easier: you. They won't go to the Discounters if they see that they're paying a fraction of the fee but getting an even smaller fraction of the service.

7. Talk about Communication as an Expression of Quality Service.

Over the last fifteen years, my company has sent out over 75,000 client-satisfaction surveys. We've probably gotten back about 20,000, and I've read just about every single one of them. It's the best, and occasionally the worst, part of my job.

Here's the most important lesson I've learned: great service means great communication. If we get a bad survey, it almost always involves complaints about a lack of communication: "My agent never called me," "My agent never returned my calls," "My agent never told me...," and grievances like that.

So when we're articulating our value proposition to our clients, we need to assert our commitment to communicating with them throughout the entire transaction. Essentially, communication becomes the seventh CORE service, as a proxy for the kind of quality attention we need to provide for the other six services. We're not only going to consult with you, help you stage your home, provide you with beautiful marketing, capably negotiate your deal, and manage the transaction—we're going to provide you with an outstanding experience throughout the whole process, particularly by staying in close contact with you.

So communication becomes the glue that holds the rest of it together—the service that starts with that initial consultation and runs through the entire process until the closing.

Modernizing the Buyer Value Proposition

Now let's talk about the value proposition for buyers.

Buyers always get short shrift, don't they? I mean, even here, I've just spent a bunch of pages talking about how to frame the services we provide to our clients, and I've talked almost exclusively about sellers. After all, buyers don't need pricing advice, or staging, or marketing—that's all seller stuff.

So let's talk about the value we provide to buyers. Sadly, we have the same problem we had with sellers: we're still advocating a value proposition that is woefully out of date.

Think about our traditional value proposition to buyers from back in the 1990s: we are the gatekeepers of information about homes for sale, we have the listings, and you need us if you want to go see them. And that was enough, since buyers couldn't find out about those listings themselves. I can remember, for example, when the inventory was literally on index cards in shoe boxes hidden away in every agents' desk drawer.

But not anymore. Not today. The idea that buyers need agents to find out what's on the market is laughable—indeed, in many cases, motivated buyers find that hot new listing before the agent does! What does that say about this traditional value proposition when a buyer calls you on a listing, demanding to meet you right at the home? Even worse, what does it say about you when you agree? You're no longer the gatekeeper, you're the door opener. If you're just someone to unlock a lockbox, or drive them to a showing, then are you really providing the kind of value that justifies your fee?

That's the message of the Discounter: why doesn't a buyer who's doing so much work on her own deserve a healthy rebate of that commission being offered to the buyer agent?

So how do we differentiate ourselves?

The key is this: start treating buyers like sellers. One of the oddest features of this industry is that we treat sellers and buyers so differently. Most agents would never take an open listing from a seller, but are willing to work with buyers who don't sign exclusive buyer representation agreements. Agents on a listing appointment will spend hours preparing a killer presentation with all sorts of glossy materials, and then they'll agree to meet a new buyer at the house with just an MLS printout. Agents submit all their listings to their broker, and ultimately to MLS, but rarely do they let anyone know the names of the buyers they're taking out.

Why the difference? Maybe it's because buyer agency is only about twenty-five years old, and we're still getting used to the idea that buyers are "clients" who deserve the same level of attention and care that sellers get. Maybe it's because the MLS has always had certain requirements to include a seller into the shared pool of inventory, which necessitated that we professionalize certain aspects of our approach to sellers—something that never developed for buyers.

Whatever the reason, it's painfully clear that, as an industry, we take a much more laissez-faire approach to our relationships with buyers. And that impacts our relationships with them. Indeed, agents often get frustrated with buyers who are notoriously fickle about committing to working exclusively with one particular agent. But in most cases, we never even ask for that type of commitment. The reason they play the field is that we never demand monogamy.

But if we're going to expect more from them, we first need to demand more from ourselves. If we aren't willing to assert ourselves, to clearly articulate the value we provide to buyers, then we deserve the perception that we're just chauffeurs and door openers.

Indeed, much of the current value proposition for buyers is the same as for sellers: buyers need consultative services, good negotiating skills, transaction management, and communication just as much as sellers do. The difference, of course, is the nature of the services we provide after the consultation and before the negotiation. Where sellers get "on the market" services, buyers get "in the market" services: where sellers need pricing advice, buyers need prequalification; where sellers need marketing, buyers need help screening properties; where sellers need staging, buyers need showing assistance.

Here are the seven CORE services that top agents (not every agent!) provide to buyers, and how we should be articulating them to our clients:

1. *Consultation.* We can start right from the beginning of the interaction with a substantive initial consultation. This would be a big change for most agents who don't give buyers even the over-rehearsed, agent-focused presentation they give to sellers. But that initial buyer appointment is the best opportunity to start providing great services that all buyers need, like a prequalification, an in-depth evolution of the kind of home they're looking for, and an overview of all the work we're going to do for them throughout the buying process. Most importantly, it sets the tone for the rest of the relationship, showing that buyer that we take them seriously

and give them the same attention and respect that we give sellers.

2. *Qualification*. Too many agents are willing to take out buyers without qualifying them. That's just not professional, and a waste of both your and your buyers' time. You cannot show a buyer a home if you don't have a good sense of how much they can afford. Even the agents who believe in prequalifying their buyers, though, often delegate the responsibility to lenders. Of course, they should certainly be enlisting a credible lender to draft a prequalification letter for their buyers, because those letters can be useful to establish bona fides with sellers. But every agent should understand the fundamentals of qualification, be able to explain how they work to their buyers, and then provide at least a general qualification guideline. It's an ideal way to build rapport and trust and to show that you're more than a door opener.

3. *Screening*. Today, buyers often come to an agent with what they think is a fairly firm grasp of the home they want, only to later end up buying something completely different. We've all seen it, so we all know how important an agent's counsel can be in helping a buyer identify her dream-home criteria. Indeed, studies show that, even today, most buyers ultimately buy a house first brought to their attention by their agent. But an agent who agrees to meet a client "at the house" is essentially reinforcing the idea that buyers don't need our guidance in the search process. Don't make that concession. Insist on meeting in person beforehand (if only for your own safety), so that you can provide that screening service as part of an initial consultation.

4. *Showing*. We all know that the showing process is more than driving and door opening, so let's be more assertive about explaining what we do in helping clients refine their search by guiding them through home tours. Too many buyers think they know what they want by looking at pictures on their tablets, but a great agent understands that preferences

often evolve once buyers start actually seeing homes. The successful agents develop the ability to ask open-ended questions that reveal what buyers are really thinking, and use that information to refine the client's search process. That's an important service we provide; we should talk about it that way.

5. *Negotiation.* As with sellers, we need to make clear that negotiation is a crucial service we provide our buyers. Indeed, buyer agents have additional work to do when they help their clients prepare an offer, because seller agents have already essentially presented an offer when they set the listing price, and probably have an accurate idea about how much their sellers want, and how much they're willing to concede. But a buyer's price range might shift depending on the individual home, so agents need to be more nimble about formulating an offer: doing a CMA to see what similar homes have sold for, researching the listing agent to get a sense of her negotiability, and counseling the client on the best approach for framing the terms.

6. *Transaction Management.* If anything, transaction man-agement is even more important for buyers, who generally have a lot more work to do from contract to closing. Why? Because they have to get a mortgage, and the mortgage process is terrible. On top of that, sellers already know the house, so they're not as stressed about what inspections, title searches, and walkthroughs might reveal. But with buyers, great agents need to coach that whole process, managing all the individual professional players (engineer, attorney, escrow, title, mortgage, insurance, home warranty) while counseling their clients through inevitable pitfalls. This is one of those times where the complexity of the transaction works in our favor—"Are you really going to try to get through that process without professional help?"

7. *Communication.* Finally, great agents keep that line of communication open as a means of providing an outstand-ing service experience. As any agent knows, buyers are more

demanding than sellers. With sellers, most of the work is front-loaded: the pricing, staging, marketing all gets done at the time the home goes on the market. After that, it's mostly a matter of maintenance. But buyers require your attention from that first consultation through to the closing, which means that an impeccable service ethic makes an even bigger difference to their experience.

And that's the CORE approach to working with buyers: treat them like sellers, articulate the value you provide to them, and then give them an unmatched service experience. Discounters cannot possibly match the suite of services a great agent can provide to a buyer.

How to Move to a Client-Oriented Approach

What we offer buyers and sellers is really quite simple: (1) we're going to get your deal done, (2) at the best possible terms, and (3) give you a great transactional experience. That's it. Everything we do, every service we provide, stems from that straightforward mission: get the deal done on the best terms with a great experience.

But implicit in that is a stronger, more important message: we're going to do it better than anyone else, particularly a low-service discount broker. Not all brokers are the same. Not all agents are the same. We're better.

So we need to modernize our value proposition to reflect the important work that we do for today's buyers and sellers. We provide value that goes well beyond the marketing we provide sellers and the inventory search we provide to buyers. So we need to make sure we're communicating that value.

In particular, we need to start emphasizing more the services we provide that Discounters cannot easily replicate at scale. They can often provide comparable marketing, since they can hire independent photographers to do the basics, and widespread distribution is available today at the click of a button. They can also sometimes do reasonable pricing given the rising quality of AVM products, although most of them simply allow the seller to price it herself. Similarly, Discounters trade on the misperception that buyers know what they want, and can do their own showings, and don't need a real agent.

But we provide many services that Discounters cannot replicate at a reasonable expense, particularly those that charge a flat fee for basic marketing services and throw the property sight unseen onto the MLS. In those cases, how can they possibly do any staging at all? How much help can they be for a buyer trying to narrow her preferences, if they've never gone on a showing with her?

Most importantly, though, we need to start emphasizing the role we play in managing our clients through the real estate transaction. The most challenging work we do starts when that buyer finds the home she wants, and that seller gets a viable offer—negotiating the deal, then guiding the client through the inspection, contract, mortgage, title, walkthrough, and closing process. The ability to deftly manage that project is what separates the great agents from their competitors. Essentially, if buyers and sellers perceive the transaction to be difficult, then use that complexity to support your argument that they need someone like you to guide them through it.

On top of all that, let's take a moment to think outside the narrow confines of the transaction. Yes, we need to do all these things to update our value proposition, but that's all about just addressing the flaws in our industry today.

But it's not enough to just survive. The real breakthrough we need will come when someone thinks outside the narrow, stifling confines of the industry as it exists today and redefines what it means to be in this business.

After all, the key in taking a client-oriented approach is to think expansively and creatively about what our clients need. So, yes, it's a good thing if we start innovating better ways to service our clients' needs in the real estate transaction, because that's the primal need our clients have. They need to buy a home. They need to sell a home. We provide them with the services to do that. We could do better. So let's.

But even then, we're still thinking like a salesperson. Our immediate reaction is to say, "What can we do better to help someone buy or sell a home?" In other words, we take the narrow view that people only need us when they're doing a transaction. Why? One simple reason: because that's when we get paid. Now, that's only natural. We're in business to make money, there's nothing wrong with that. But isn't it a little self-serving to think that the only time clients need us is when they're doing a transaction? Isn't that thinking as much about our needs—the need for a commission—as their needs?

The problem is that this confined and industry-centric view of what consumers need blinds us to the idea that people might have nontransactional needs that we're not addressing. That's why we turned the "what is my home worth?" question into our offer for a "Free CMA!" We treated it narrowly as a way to generate a transaction and missed the relationship-building opportunity that Zillow seized.

We have to flip that mentality—stop thinking about ourselves and our needs and start thinking creatively about what clients need. And when I say clients, I don't just mean people who are buying or selling a home right now. I mean everyone.

In other words, what do people need from us, and how can we give it to them? Because once we start thinking outside the transaction, we can think about all sorts of real estate needs that we're currently not meeting, like these:

The Market. People need to keep track of what's going on in the local real estate market: is it up, down, hot, cold, whatever. After all, not everyone is in the stock market, or the bond market, but we're all in the real estate market. Everyone lives somewhere.

Neighborhood. More granularly, people also need to know what's happening with listings and sales in their local neighborhood. When they see a sign go up, they want to know how much the house is selling for. Yes, they can find that out by looking online, but most people aren't in the habit of doing real estate searches online when they're not in the market. So they don't get around to it much. And they're even more curious when the sign goes down, because they want to know what the house sold for—and that's not information that's readily available online.

Real Estate. But beyond just local property values and neighborhood sales, people need to know what's happening with regard to real estate generally. What's happening with the national market? What about the regulatory environment? Will tax changes affect home ownership? We know people have a keen general interest in real estate—otherwise, HGTV and all those home improvement shows wouldn't be so popular.

Property Management. People need advice about property management: how to file a grievance about their taxes, what schedule of routine maintenance should they follow, and that sort of thing. They also constantly need a resource for professional referrals for everything relating to the home: landscapers, alarm system providers, plumbers, electricians, general contractors, pest control, and other service providers. Who better to advise them about managing their property than a real estate professional?

Home Improvement Advice. Every homeowner needs professional real estate guidance anytime they're considering making home improvements. Should they renovate their kitchen, or add a bathroom, or build a pool, or finish their basement? How should they do the work to get the best return on their investment? No one should ever do any kind of home improvement without at least considering the impact on their property values. Who else can help them do that?

Community. Finally, people need to know what's going on in their local community. This could involve changes that might impact property values: new businesses coming in, changes in zoning, property tax impacts, and so on. But it also means having a resource to keep them informed about local events, programs, services, and things like that—and who better than a real estate agent wired into the local community, who has a vested interest in promoting all the great reasons people should live there? Traditionally, real estate professionals have always taken a leadership role in their local communities, precisely because they literally "live off the land"—we make our income based on the desirability of the markets we service, so it's in our interest to promote them as much as possible.

What's the point? That consumers have all sorts of real estate needs that aren't being met, or at least aren't being aggressively pursued by our industry. Why? Because no one is going to pay us for keeping them updated about what's happening in the market or the community, or for answering their questions about property management or home improvement. So why would we invest time, money, and energy in providing these kinds of nontransactional services?

Because no one ever paid for a Zestimate either. And yet Zillow made it work.

And so can we. We have to stop thinking transactionally and start thinking relationally. Yes, people pay us for a transaction, but that's not the only time they need us. They need us all the time. All. The. Time.

Why is this important? Because if we can build relationships with consumers outside of the transactions, they're more likely to forgo the lure of the Discounters when it's time for them to do a transaction.

This isn't a revolutionary way of thinking about real estate. Most agents understand that this is a relationship business, and brilliant educators like Brian Buffini and Tom Ferry have long preached the gospel of building a dependable referral business by aggressively reaching out to your database with these kinds of nontransactional services.

But let's take the idea even a step further than that. These non-transactional real estate services are just an example of how we can broaden our perspective on what people should expect from us. After all, we're still just talking about real estate services that relate to home ownership or management. What about renters, landlords, and investors?

Even then, we're still thinking within the narrow confines of real estate services. What if we took a broader view and started thinking about that traditional role we have as stewards of a community? Where could we go with that? How could we create services that would help our local communities be better places to live, which would not only make our jobs selling homes easier but maybe create the kind of creatively fertile environment that would lead to the next big breakthrough, the next Zillow?

That's where we need to be. And maybe the first place to start is by improving the real estate transaction we inflict on people.

Key #4: Improve the Transactional Experience: Fast. Cheap. Good.

I REMEMBER SEEING A FRAMED FLYER at a local copier when I was in college: *You can get it fast, cheap, and good. Pick any two.*

In other words, you can get it fast and cheap, but it won't be good. Or you can get it fast and good, but it won't be cheap. And, of course, you can get it cheap and good, but it won't be fast.

I didn't know it at the time, but it's called the Project Management Triangle, a model for looking at how to allocate resources in project management. I've always loved the concept, which can be applied to almost any situation where you're trying to express the cost of trade-offs when you can't have everything.

Like, if you're looking for a job, you can get one that has great pay, great hours, and great work—pick any two. Because only people like George Clooney, Derek Jeter, and Beyoncé get all three.

Looking for a spouse? You can get money, looks, and personality—pick any two! Because, well, again, George Clooney, Derek Jeter, Beyoncé...

So what does the triangle have to do with disruption? Basically, Disruptors are usually trying to change the existing paradigm. They look for an industry that is confined by the triangle—that is making consumers pick any two—and they try to find a way to give them all three. Or, even better, they look for truly dysfunctional industries that might be making consumers pick any one, which are much easier targets. Or even an industry that doesn't let people pick anything at all.

Think about taxis. For eons, consumers accepted the "pick any two" limitations of the taxi and limo industry:

- You could get it cheap and fast—flag a taxi on the street—but sitting in the average cab wasn't a particularly good experience.

- Or you could get it cheap and good by calling for car service—but you'd be sitting on your phone on hold, and then waiting until a car was available.

- Or you could get it fast and good by calling a high-end limo—but that certainly wouldn't be cheap.

And then came Uber—a luxury car service on demand, priced to be competitive with the taxi on the street. Fast. Cheap. Good. That's why Uber has become the archetype for modern disruption companies. Uber found a way to break that triangle and provide a surpassing client experience.

Now, just to be clear, Uber is really only able to do that because it loses a lot of money while it tries to establish market dominance. So we're all getting cheap Uber rides subsidized by the generous people at various venture capital firms. It's certainly nice of them. Lots of Disruptors, including some in the real estate industry itself, are like that—they're able to do things that established businesses, which need to actually make money, cannot. It's nice when you're a consumer getting cheap rides, next-day delivery, and people who do your grocery shopping for you; less nice when you're a competitor who doesn't have venture capital money to set on fire.

But the larger point is this: Disruptors try to break that triangle and provide consumers with a better experience than is available from the dominant industry model.

So let's think about that with regard to real estate. Are we providing a service that is fast, cheap, and good and giving consumers the opportunity to pick any two? Heck, with today's real estate transaction, are we giving them a chance to even pick one?

- *Are we fast?* No. Selling a home takes forever.

- *Are we cheap?* We could argue about the relative value of traditional real estate commission structures, but I think it's fair to say that we're not considered to be particularly cheap.

- *Are we good?* At our best, we definitely are. Great real estate agents provide an amazing service to their clients. But we all know that most of the agents in the industry aren't particularly good at their jobs. So even this is a little hit or miss.

Yikes! One out of three, at best. No wonder venture capitalists keep pouring money into our Disruptors looking to find a model that is faster, cheaper, and better than what we're providing in the traditional brokerage industry.

So how do we overcome this challenge? As I've argued throughout this book, we need to flip our sales-dominated mentality and start focusing our energies on providing our clients with a better transactional experience. We have to stop thinking about sales and about our own needs and focus on the needs of our clients.

For example, consider how the industry has approached innovation over the past twenty years. Think about all the fancy new tools and programs that the industry has created in this current technological era. Now, think about how few of them are intended to actually make a client's experience better. Whenever we develop a new innovation or technology—website features, direct mail, email, social media, video, digital photography—we immediately adapt it exclusively for the purpose of haranguing consumers to try to generate sales. We've put almost no energy, and little money, into actually improving the client experience: simplifying the real estate transaction, providing a communication platform, implementing true project management, or just making it easier for agents to do their jobs.

Take, for example, the average real estate website. Over the last twenty years, since our website first starting giving consumers access to MLS inventory, we've made dramatic improvements in the display of our listings. We've added multiple high-resolution photos, videos, 3-D walkthroughs, mapping, satellite imagery, walk scores, school reports, you name it. All these state-of-the-art bells and whistles are designed to do one thing: attract shoppers and get them to click on the "find out more" button.

That's how we've built our websites: for shoppers. Not even buyers, shoppers. Because once those shoppers become buyers, once they're actually working with an agent and they've found a home they want to purchase, the sites become virtually useless. Why? Because the sites don't provide any actual services that would guide the buyer through the sales process. Once shoppers become buyers and get into contract, they have no reason to even visit the website—other than to generate buyer's remorse when they see something new come on the market.

Indeed, our websites provide virtually no services to half our clients—the sellers! Yes, we list their home online, with all the fancy pictures and videos, which is a nice service for our sellers. But with all the money and energy we spend, do we give our sellers any real reason to visit the website? Can they get updates on their deal? Information on their competition? Help through their transactional process? No. They can only check to make sure their home is listed and that the pictures are up-to-date.

Essentially, all of the creative, innovative energy of the last twenty years has been designed to do one thing: generate leads from websites. Now we're seeing even more energy (and venture capital money) going to improve our conversion rate of these online leads— all to justify years of investments devoted solely to driving eyeballs and clicks.

Why? Because of the original sin, we have this sales-exclusive mind-set about the industry, and because we think of real estate agents as only salespeople, all our innovative energy goes into generating leads. We have to flip that mind-set and think creatively and expansively about what our clients need from us and how we can give it to them.

This isn't going to be easy. Some of these wannabe Disruptors are targeting the broken transaction because selling a home is inherently hard, and buying a home is even harder. We just have a lot of moving parts in the transaction, the kind of complexity that you don't have, say, in retail sales or hospitality.

What's worse, we don't control all the moving parts. Even in situations where we do an amazing job helping a buyer get into contract, we're still relying on an array of third-party service providers to get that buyer to closing: inspection engineers, lawyers, title readers, escrow agents, mortgage lenders, home insurance providers. As an industry, we need to start thinking like Disruptors. They're all looking at the real estate transaction from the outside and trying to find ways to make it cheaper, faster, and better.

So why can't we do that? We know that transaction better than anyone else. We know the pain points. We know the inefficiencies. We know what our clients really need. So why don't we take that immense amount of knowledge and use it to disrupt our own industry?

Here are seven suggestions for how we could improve the real estate transaction, from that first consultation to the final closing—and even beyond.

1. Embrace Instant Buyer Programs.

Here's the hottest pitch in real estate over the past year: *Wouldn't it be great if you could sell your home in a week? Just go online, put in your address, get a bunch of immediate cash offers, accept one, and call the moving company—because you're out!*

That's what consumers are starting to hear from companies like Opendoor and the Zillow "Instant Offers" program (and by the time you read this, probably a bunch more). The basic idea is simple. These companies have investors ready to buy homes for cash to either rent or flip and are valuing those homes using an online, automated valuation model. They don't need a mortgage, which eliminates the biggest delay in the real estate industry. And they run their own title operations, so they can secure insurance in a few days.

Their seductive message is that the homeowner can avoid all the horrors of the real estate experience: cleaning and staging the home, living through open houses and showings, dealing with offers, and then waiting through the endless mortgage and title process. Just type in your address, get a great offer, and pack it up.

Faster. Cheaper. Better.

These companies have made a big splash in the last year or so, getting a lot of venture capital money and attention—and driving the Doubters crazy. Indeed, when Zillow announced its Instant Offers program in 2017, over 25,000 agents signed a petition to the National Association of REALTORS demanding that Zillow stop the program. That's a lot of angst.

But why is everyone so worried? For one thing, if you look a little deeper at these programs, you start to see holes. They're certainly fast, of course—that's the dominant feature of the model. But are they cheap? Are they good?

Like with most things that sound too good to be true, there's a catch. Yes, you can sell your home in a week, but it's going to be expensive. That whole disruptive business model is built on a trade-off between convenience and cost. Not only are these immediate offers usually well below true market value, but these companies also charge an administrative fee or transaction fee that amounts to 6 to 12 percent of the sales price. In other words, the fees associated with taking those instant offers are actually as high, or higher, than the typical real estate commission. And the sales price is usually a lot lower.

So they've got the fast part down, and you might even say that they provide a good experience if they get you out in a week. But not so much with the cheap, not if sellers are taking significantly less than they'd get from the traditional industry model.

So why would anyone use one of these services? Some people are, well, stupid, and they make bad decisions. Can't do much about them. But mostly, it's that others really hate the process of selling a home, and they're willing to take less (although I wonder how many of them realize how much less) to get it done quickly. They're willing to pick any two—fast and good.

You've probably done the same thing, if you think about it. You've picked up milk at the convenience store, rather than schlep to the supermarket, even though you know it's more expensive. You've traded in your car at a dealership, rather than try to sell it yourself, even though you could probably get more in a private sale. These instant sellers are making the same calculation you did, albeit with a lot more money at stake.

That's why I'm not so sure that these instant programs will do more than service a relatively small part of the market of sellers who need the convenience of a quick sale: people going through a divorce, executors of estates, relocation companies. But even if you agree with me, that's no reason to be complacent.

Certainly, the smart people running Open Home, Instant Offers, and their ilk might find ways to reduce that transaction fee or raise their purchase prices, narrowing their margins but providing a service that would appeal to a much larger audience of sellers. And even if they remain niche players, that doesn't mean the traditional industry should just sit back and hope for the best.

Instead, why don't we embrace the concept, like Brad Inman has argued? After all, lots of brokers and agents make similar, if not as slick, offers—"If we can't sell your house, we'll buy it!" Heck, the ERA franchise has had that kind of program for years. Think about what you'd have to do to disrupt the Disruptor, to create a better, faster, cheaper version of what the instant buyer companies are offering.

First, you need a good-sized set of institutional investors who are looking to purchase well-priced homes at a discount, can make quick decisions, and can close immediately. How do we find them? Obviously, they're out there, because Zillow was able to corral a bunch of them quickly when they felt threatened by Opendoor.

Second, you need a system for submitting those properties to the investors for quick decisions. Most likely, the investors are already using an automated value model in formulating their offers, so you just need a way to submit these listings to the buyers quickly and efficiently. This seems like a relatively routine programming challenge of taking a property data set, matching it to public records and MLS data to feed the AVM, and then transmitting it in an established format to a set of recipients. Not trivial, but not Project Upstream, either.

Third, you need a good-sized marketing program that rivals what Opendoor and others have been able to do with all their venture capital. Well, how about a million agents in every neighborhood in the country advertising and promoting their instant buyer program as an alternative to their standard (and modernized!) value proposition. It might go something like this: *Okay, we have two ways that we can market your home: First, the marketing program, which takes some work and can require a few months, but will help you get the best price; or, second, our instant offer program that can have you out of your home in a week and can still get you a pretty good price. So which makes more sense for you?*

Indeed, I'm not so sure that an alternate instant buyer program needs to get to a closing in less than a week. That's an extravagant promise from some of these start-ups, but is it necessary? Most sellers probably don't need to move quite that quickly. My guess is that the most attractive part of the instant programs is the quick contract, avoiding all the preparation of the home, the market time, the showings, and all that. If someone in the industry came up with a viable program that got you out of your home in thirty days, I think that would be competitive.

So why don't we? Instant offers is a good idea, so let's steal it.

2. End Search Chaos.

In a lot of ways, real estate search is in its golden age. As an industry, we've now been providing consumers with online access to real estate inventory for over twenty years, and we've never given them so many useful features and so many options for looking for a home.

But the sheer number of websites and apps that provide search is creating a new problem: search chaos. Even with all the millions of dollars and untold hours that we've spent refining and improving real estate search, we're still providing our clients with a disjointed and even chaotic experience.

Here's what I mean. Let's say I'm a home buyer who started gingerly looking for a new home a few months ago and created an account on a portal like Zillow. Over the course of a few months, I set up some automated searches that send me email alerts about new properties hitting the market or significant changes to my saved properties.

Then, once I got serious, I started working with an agent. Now, not only am I looking on my own, using my Zillow account, but I'm starting to get email alerts from my agent for properties she's finding for me—either manually or through her own automated searches. And if I click on the links in her emails, I'm not going to my Zillow account. Instead, I'm going to either her website, or her broker's website, or her RealScout listing, or even her MLS public-facing portal. And if I want to save that listing, I'm saving it on that system, not on my Zillow account—unless I go to the trouble of opening up Zillow, finding that listing, and then saving it there.

So now I'm getting email alerts from both Zillow and my agent, and I'm visiting at least two different sites when I click on the links in those emails—and that's assuming that I was using only Zillow when I started my search. But maybe I was leery about whether Zillow had all the listings, so I was also using Realtor.com, or Trulia, or Homesnap, or my broker's website. The more websites I use, the more redundant email alerts I'm getting and the more places where I have saved searches and saved listings.

That's chaos. Why? Because none of these systems talk to each other. My broker's site doesn't share information with Zillow, which doesn't share with Realtor.com, which doesn't share with my agent's MLS account.

Even worse, think about all the people who buy homes with a spouse or a partner? Most search sites allow only a single log-in account, so if I'm looking with my wife, we have to share the credentials. But that also means we have to share the email account that's getting the alerts. Even worse, how do I keep track of what she's doing, and how does she keep track of what I'm doing? I log into my account and find a whole bunch of saved properties I've never seen before.

How do we solve this? One system could win out and become the standard. You might say, "Well, that's easy. Zillow is winning the battle for search, everyone will just use Zillow. No more chaos." Except that Zillow's dominance is largely at the early stage of that buyer's search process (the shopping stage).

Zillow is outstanding at attracting those early shoppers, but it loses its hold on people who start working more intensely with an agent and get closer to the purchase point. And that agent is almost certainly not using Zillow—so if that buyer wants the benefit of an agent who is bird-dogging listings for her, she's going to end up in chaos if she splits her attention between Zillow and the agent's suggestions. And even though Zillow might be the search leader right now, millions of people are still using their broker websites, or other portals, or working exclusively through their agent's MLS email alerts.

So how do we reduce chaos without resorting to a search monopoly? These systems need to find ways to talk to one another—to develop a universal standard for saving searches and properties so that they port from one site to the other. Let the consumer search on one site, the agent on another, and let them collaborate on a third.

Luckily, we are seeing efforts to standardize different aspects of the transaction. For example, the Real Estate Standards Organization (RESO) has promulgated a standard for saved searches, favorites, and all the other search elements that is supposed to be adopted by all MLS systems by mid-2018 and followed by all the competing vendors. Project Upstream has developed a universal platform for listing data entry. And the Broker Portal, which is now being launched through Homesnap, integrates consumer search with agent search.

At the very least, though, we have to change our mind-set with regard to search. Right now, everyone's competing for eyeballs, because we all want to capture leads that we can send to our agents or advertisers. But it's that very competition that's creating the chaos. We need to start thinking of search almost as a utility, with common carriers, and allow for more collaborative search across platforms. I save a property on Zillow, and it's saved when I go back to my broker's site.

Moreover, we need to rethink the utility of email as a way of providing client alerts. Emails that get buried inside inboxes crammed with junk is just a terrible way of managing a search process, particularly in markets where an immediate response to a new listing might be necessary. And the answer isn't to start texting them incessantly either. We need a new paradigm for managing search. Wouldn't it be exciting if the solution came from inside the real estate industry, rather than outside?

3. Centralize and Improve Transaction Communication.

Transaction management has long been the elusive Moby Dick of the real estate industry, the great white whale that we're obsessed with mastering. And that's an apt analogy, because in the end Captain Ahab harpoons Moby and turns him into sushi and a lovely wall ornament, just like we're eventually going to find a seamless transaction management program that will work for everyone! (Oh, wait, maybe not the best analogy, because apparently Moby Dick ends up dragging Ahab to his death. Spoiler alert!)

Or maybe it is the right analogy, because perhaps we've been going about this all wrong. For years, we've been trying to find one transaction management platform that can do everything from that initial listing or buyer agreement, to offer and acceptance, through the mortgage and title process, and all the way to closing. Then on top of that, we've been looking for something that's affordable for both agents and brokers, fully integrated with the dominant mortgage and title processing systems, universally accepted throughout the industry so we don't have competing systems creating chaos, completely digitalized, and simple to learn and to use for the average agent. That's a lot to ask, and maybe if we keep trying to achieve the impossible, we're going to end up in our own watery grave.

But maybe a full-featured transaction management platform is not what we need. Maybe we've been trying to do too much. Maybe we should stop thinking about managing our transactions and just focus on improving the communication around our transaction. We don't necessarily need one system that manages the transaction. That's simply impossible when a real estate deal involves multiple institutional players (agent, lawyer/escrow, mortgage, title, insurance) who are each using their own uniquely customized processing systems. We're asking too much for all these systems to work together.

Indeed, agents don't really need to manage the transaction. They're not really managing that loan processor, or title reader, or attorney, or escrow closer. Rather, they're just supposed to be staying on top of what's happening with each aspect of the transaction and communicating that to the client.

So what we need is a better way of making that communication transparent—in other words, systems that accommodate all these different processes and provide a more open, fluid, and even automatic set of transactional updates for clients. We know what clients are curious about—they want to know what's happening with their listing, or the status of their mortgage/title/escrow. Why can't we create automated systems that allow them to track their status?

Think about what happens when you order something from Amazon. Amazon doesn't deliver packages itself; it contracts delivery services through third-party companies like UPS or FedEx. But you can track the status of your delivery right on your Amazon order page, because the delivery companies feed that information directly to Amazon's systems. That's what I mean by communication management.

But if you have a problem with the delivery, or want to make any changes, you can't do that on Amazon—you have to go to UPS or FedEx directly. That's transaction management.

That's what we need in real estate: a transaction *communication* platform, not a transaction *management* platform. We need a centralized platform that can simply pull data streams from all the disparate industry systems and tie them together into a comprehensive update and monitoring process. And it's certainly a lot easier to connect those systems by using API's to simply feed information to a central communication platform than it would be to actually integrate them.

Simply put, we don't need better transaction management. We just need better communication. We improve communication, we improve the transaction.

4. Adopt Better Communication Tools Than Email and Text.

While we're at it, let's try to get rid of using email and texting for client communication during a real estate transaction. Better tools are out there, so let's use them. Here's why.

I've read about 20,000 client surveys over the past fifteen years, and I'm grateful that the vast majority of them describe positive experiences. But if we get a bad result, it's almost always due to one very specific problem: a lack of communication. Too many clients feel as if they don't know what's going on during their transaction. Why? In addition to the lack of a comprehensive communication platform, I think it's because they're relying on back-and-forth emails, phone calls, and text messages with their agents.

You would think that in this era, when we have access to so many forms of interaction, we would be able to communicate better. But we don't. Part of the problem is that we almost have too many ways to message one another, too many places to check for updates. Agents are basically overwhelmed by the sheer number of messages that they get each day.

Even worse, think about the clients who get inundated with email messages throughout the entire process. They start with constant property alerts while they're shopping for a home. Then, once they're in contract, they're navigating through updates and requests from all those other transactional players, which come in through email, text, Facebook messages, phone calls—with sometimes repeat messages going to multiple accounts, particularly if they're buying with a spouse or partner. How are they supposed to keep track of all that, when these important emails are buried in a mountain of spam and personal stuff?

The problem is we're still using these communication technologies that aren't well-designed for managing large projects like a real estate transaction. We don't usually think of the real estate transaction as a classic management project, but that's exactly what it is: a project with a definitive goal involving demanding stakeholders and requiring the skills of a variety of diverse contributors.

Indeed, as projects go, a real estate transaction is particularly challenging because it involves high stakes and a particularly complicated environment. Agents are essentially project managers tasked by clients with managing that complex process, organizing all the service providers, and driving the transaction through to closing.

If a real estate transaction is really a project, then we should be looking to the vast array of concepts, resources, and tools available to help agents manage that process. We need to get agents working with general collaboration tools like Slack, Basecamp, industry-specific programs like Amitree's Folio, or even private social networks as a means of improving client communication.

Even better, we should be adapting these project management tools for the specific needs of the real estate transaction. Not only do these services provide a more seamless communication experience, but they also preserve all those communiques to provide a more comprehensive documentary record of the entire transaction.

Most importantly, we should stop using basic email. Everyone hates email. Let's find a better way to communicate.

5. Be More Proactive about the Mortgage Process.

If we're going to improve the transactional experience, we have to do something about the mortgage experience. Why? Because the mortgage process is the worst part of the transaction. It's the source of most of our buyers' frustration, and where most deals end up bogging down.

That angst reflects on us. You might work with a buyer for months and months, patiently refining their search process while you look for the perfect home, expertly negotiating their deal, and then adroitly facilitating them into contract. They absolutely love you, and for good reason.

Then they try to get their mortgage, and everything goes to hell. They never know what's going on, no one calls them back, they get asked for documents again and again, and so on. They get frustrated and angry and come out of the closing with a terrible taste in their mouths. Then you show up with a plant and hope that they'll give you a stunning review because of all the good work you did months and months ago.

We need to take greater ownership of the mortgage experience, which is something we've never done. Trying to improve the transaction without influencing the mortgage is like trying to provide a delicious meal without influencing the chef. The lender is the most important player in this game.

So how do we improve the mortgage process? Unfortunately, the best we can do is nibble around the edges. The real frustrations in the mortgage process come from their vast internal bureaucracies and lack of automation. For example, how is it that a start-up like Updater can connect with my banks to do my change of address automatically, but when I apply for a mortgage, I have to get my printed bank statements, scan them, and then email them to my processor? Why can't banks get all those annoying forms completely automatically, or at least digitally? Why haven't they automated the routine and mechanical parts of their underwriting processes? We're so worried about disruption, yet the big banks act as if they can continue to give horrible experiences to their mortgage applicants. It's amazing.

Brokers and agents need to be more aggressive in pushing banks to streamline their operations. I get that they're risk-averse to making changes in their systems, but their processes are so bad that they're creating artificial incentives for sellers to opt for instant offer sales simply to avoid working with a buyer who has to get a mortgage. They're catalyzing the potential for disruption of the entire industry. So we need to start putting more pressure on them to get better.

But we should also be focusing on what's within our control, such as these factors.

First, let's start with helping our buyers be more proactive in the loan process. Get them preapproved by a reputable and credible lender. Get them started in credit repair while they're shopping for a home, rather than waiting until they've already submitted an application. Give them a list of all the documents they're going to need right at the first showing, so they start collecting and saving paperwork immediately. In other words, spread the pain out.

Second, since one of the most significant sources of delays in the process is a failed appraisal, be aggressive in providing appraisers with sound comparable market information. Obviously, we used to be able to get much more involved in the appraisal process before the post-crash reforms, but in most states we're still allowed to provide information (such as comps or a list of improvements) that could help an appraiser avoid making negligent valuation mistakes. Too many agents only get involved in that process after the appraisal comes in light, which is too late.

Third, agents should be driving as much business as they can to a lender that they can exert some influence over to ensure more responsiveness and accountability. Real estate agents have this antiquated rule-of-three idea that they should give a list of at least three lenders to avoid liability, which probably comes from some NAR-sponsored overly risk-averse pablum.

That's nonsense. For one thing, even if your referral screws things up, you're not going to be professionally liable. Making a recommendation is not the same as agreeing to be a guarantor of another provider's services. In addition, if you were going to be liable (which, again, you're not!), you're not going to be able to defend yourself by saying, "Well, my client chose the wrong name on the list I gave them." That name was still on the list, right?

So stop it with the rule of three and make it a rule of one—strongly encourage your clients to use the best lender you have and provide as much business to that lender as you can. Who's your best lender? Obviously, you want someone who has competitive rates, offers a good range of products for your market, and provides an outstanding client-service experience.

But just as important, you want someone who will answer your phone calls when you have a problem. That's why you should be driving as much business as possible to that one lender—because that gives you influence. Your loan officer will return your calls. You'll get to know the processor, maybe even the primary underwriters, so you know whom to call when things bog down. That's how you get things done.

That's why, for example, I always encourage agents to focus on their broker's affiliated lender—assuming that lender has good rates, product, and service. It's not just about the money, it's about controlling the process.

Full disclosure: I own an affiliated mortgage company, so take this as you wish. But here's the thing: if my agents recommend some third-party lender, and that lender screws up, who are they going to call? Are they going to get the head of some national bank on the phone? But if my agent recommends my affiliates, and then has a problem, that agent can call me. And get me on the phone. And yell at me. And I have to listen. And then I go yell at people too.

But even if it's not your affiliate, you should drive as much as you can to a single lender because that gives you more influence. We should be doing the same thing across the industry at large. Ultimately, we're never going to control the mortgage process. That's in the hands of the lenders. But we could be doing more to exert our collective influence over those lenders to get them to get better at their part of the transaction. We need to be willing to make strong recommendations to our clients about their lending choices. And we need to stop supporting lenders who do bad work just because they buy our broker open house lunch.

6. Help Our Clients Actually Move.

First impressions count. So do last impressions.

We're darned good at first impressions. Agents tend to come into that first client meeting well-prepared with slick materials and snappy patter, since they're still in their solicitation mode. They're working to get the business.

But we're sadly bad at that last impression. By then, we've been working with those clients for months, and we're all naturally tired of one another. Most real estate deals limp into the finish line: everyone's so exhausted from the long transactional process that they just want it to be over.

As an agent, you don't have a great way to finish. If you're in an attorney state, you try to show up at the closing, but everyone's so stressed out that they're not in the right mind-set to fully appreciate you (or the closing gift you might have schlepped over). And if you're in an escrow state, it's even worse—the deal just closes, voila! without any ceremonial moment at all.

So our last impression is either giving a client a bottle of champagne or a plant or whatever while they're in the middle of a stressful legal procedure, or making a phone call after escrow closes to offer a belated congratulations.

Even worse, we have traditionally defined our client responsibilities as ending the moment that title transfers. That makes sense, I guess. We were hired to sell their house, they sold. We were hired to find them a house, they found one. And we know the job is done, since we just got paid.

But that's sort of thinking like a salesperson, right? It's defining our clients' needs in reference to when we get paid. It's thinking transactionally, not relationally. And that's not helping us provide a better transaction. After all, clients come away from their long deal with that last impression. Even if you did an outstanding job through the buying and selling process, you might end up leaving a bad taste in their mouth at the very end.

Let's go back to the CORE concept: do clients have needs after the closing? And could we service those needs? If we think expansively about what they need, and how we could help them, we find all sorts of ways that we could be enhancing those relationships.

For one thing, actually moving is its own separate circle of hell. Traditionally, we haven't involved ourselves in the physical move. For example, we've seen real estate brokers branch out into all sorts of affiliated businesses like mortgage, title, escrow, insurance, property management, and all that, but I know very few brokers who own a moving company. Why? Because the margins aren't great, but the headaches are.

As a broker, I look at moving and think, "Okay, so now I have to deal with angry phone calls every time someone breaks a lamp on the truck? No thanks!" Hawking loans is enough trouble as it is.

But even if we don't want to own the moving company, that doesn't mean we can't be more helpful in guiding our clients through the move. At the very least, nonfinancial affiliate referral arrangements that allow you to recommend a small set of vetted movers who will give discounts, benefits, or other incentives to your clients in return for those consistent recommendations seems to make sense. We shouldn't just be handing them the yellow pages (alert: outdated old man reference!) and wishing them luck.

Similarly, why shouldn't we be more involved in helping our clients get started in their new home? They need utilities, internet, phone, and alarm systems. They need to execute myriad change-of-address forms. Again, at the very least, providing clients with a set of resources to help them through that process would be a way to maintain that relationship through the move-in process—which, incidentally, is when they usually fill out client-satisfaction surveys.

For example, we had a measurably positive impact on our surveys when we started enlisting all our buyers into Updater, which is a free service that helps people through the change-of-address process and some other move-in frustrations. They love Updater, so they tend to come away with better impressions of us as well.

The point is, our clients' real estate journeys don't end at the closing table. So our jobs shouldn't end there either.

7. Better Educate Our Clients.

Finally, let's do a better job educating our clients about what to expect in their real estate transaction.

We forget how little most of our clients know about buying or selling a home. Yes, we tend to be solicitous and attentive to the needs of our first-time home buyers, because they come to us pretty much admitting they have no idea what they're doing. And in most cases they're young, they're renters, they stand out for their inexperience. But what about the rest of our clients?

For example, we never really think about how many of our sell-side clients are first-time home sellers. Yes, if they're homeowners, they've gone through a real estate transaction, so they think they have an idea of what to expect. But many of them have only been through the purchase, not the sale. And we all know that those are two very different experiences. That's what makes them so dangerous, because they know what they know, but they don't know what they don't know.

On top of all that, even our experienced clients have probably only been through the transactional experience once or twice in their lives, and in many cases they bought or sold years ago in a totally different industry and market. They may have bought their last home before the internet, so they're not prepared when you put pictures of their bedroom online for everyone to see—with a map showing people how to get there. Or maybe they bought before buyer agency, and they are still under the impression that the agent showing the home works for them as a subagent.

In other words, virtually all of our clients come to the real estate transaction without really knowing what to expect, or even worse with a head full of outdated expectations and misinformation. Therefore, we need to do a better job of educating them about what to expect and to prepare them for the frustrations of the transactional process.

On the buy side, that means talking a client through the entire process right from the beginning, showing them how to set up a proper online search, explaining prequalification, and especially preparing them for what they'll need during the mortgage process. Too often, we treat buyers like timid little birds gingerly pecking seeds out of our hands, worried that being honest with them will spook them and make them fly away. Far too often, we indulge them (and ourselves) in the fantasy of how much home they can afford, rather than taking them through a proper prequalification process.

Similarly, on the sell-side, we need to prepare sellers for the challenges of being on the market. That means explaining the detailing and staging process, and how important it is to maintain the condition of the home during the entire time it's on the market. It also means making sure they understand the depth of the marketing that we do in the internet era, which will help avoid, for example, angry calls from clients who were not aware that their expensive artwork was going to show up in 3-D walkthrough videos.

How do we better educate our clients? We can't just rely on agents explaining things in initial meetings with clients. Yes, we need to do more of that, but people don't retain a lot of that information. So we need to be providing clients with materials they can go back to again and again to reinforce the advice and information we're giving them.

For example, my company has put out what we call the Orientation Guide, which is a series of "explainers" that guide buyers and sellers through the entire transactional process. They're helpful, but even better would be a set of short explainer videos, simply because no one reads anything anymore. You don't need to go out and create your own materials. You can find a lot of good stuff in bookstores, or on the internet, or provided by people like David Knox, who puts out excellent explainer videos.

Similarly, we're seeing some real estate start-ups move into the space, trying to find ways to better guide clients through the transactional process. Amitree, for example, has a rigorously comprehensive and customizable set of transactional checklists that both agents and clients can access online, and which can be incorporated into your gmail account through their Folio product. And that's just one way to collaborate with clients on the process and give them a sense of what they need to do, and what's up ahead.

Indeed, as professionals who deal with real estate every single day, we forget sometimes how stressful buying or selling a home can be. I've joked before that all real estate agents should be legally compelled to buy and sell their homes every five years, just to remind them of how painful the process is.

What's funny is that buyers and sellers are generally miserable at different points of the transaction. At the beginning, buyers love the process. After all, they're shopping, and who doesn't love shopping? They get to go into other people's homes, make snarky comments on the décor, and imagine themselves living there.

Meanwhile, sellers are miserable, because living in a home that's for sale is no fun. You have to get rid of half your stuff, keep the place clean, and then endure showing after showing—and all those snarky comments about your décor!

Then, once you get an accepted offer, everything flips. Now, buyers are miserable because they now have to go through the mortgage process, which is a nightmare. And sellers are loving life because they get to live like normal people again, sort of like a couple getting back to their regular diets after they slimmed down for their wedding.

The point is, at different times during the transaction, people are miserable. It's unavoidable. So we need to do a better job preparing them for that. Forewarned is forearmed.

Which Do We Pick?

Better. Faster. Cheaper. I don't know that we can ever build an industry that embraces all three of the triangle virtues because we will probably never be the cheapest option. And I don't know that we want to be.

But we could always be better. We could provide our clients with a superior transaction, one that eliminates so many of the pain points that undermine the experience and create opportunities for Disruptors.

Surely we could be faster. Maybe not "we can transfer title in five days" fast, because that kind of immediacy usually comes at a severe cost to the seller. But we have to harness the power of modern technology to streamline the closing process and give our clients the experience they need and deserve.

Again, this institutional change is not going to be easy. But we have to try. If we don't improve the transactional experience, someone else will do it for us.

Key #5: Stop Doubting Ourselves: The Confessions of a Realtophile

SHE TRIED TO FSBO HER OWN HOME.

Not a big deal, right? I mean, it happens all the time.

Except that she was one of our own agents.

Seriously. It was actually kind of ludicrous that she thought no one would find out. But, of course, once she put that sign in her yard and listed with an online FSBO service, she started getting agents prospecting her with cold calls—the old "how long do you plan on waiting until you hire an agent to sell your home?"

And, of course, once they found out that she was an agent, they all squealed on her.

So we sat her down and explained why this was such a terrible idea: how she would be sending a dreadful message to her clients, how she needed to demonstrate that she believed in the value of the services she was paid to provide. Indeed, our firm's policy is that agents selling their own home get almost all of the company dollar back in the deal, so she wouldn't even be paying any significant listing commission. But that wasn't enough for her—she refused to even offer out a commission to buyer agents.

She wouldn't budge. She was adamant that since she was a professional agent, she didn't need the market's help to sell her home. She could do it herself.

She doesn't work for us anymore.

The Disruptors and Discounters are trying to destroy us from the outside, but the biggest threat we face comes from the inside: the Doubters—the self-hating agents who don't believe in the value provided by the industry. The ones who reek of desperation at every listing presentation, who cut their commission whenever the seller says boo. The ones who complain about the market this year, just like they complained about the last market, and the one before that. The ones who are sure that our days are numbered, that it's just a matter of time before the Disruptors and Discounters take us down.

They're wrong, of course. Even if they were right, though, they'd still be wrong. Because even if you're as concerned as I am about the challenges posed by the Disruptors and Discounters, you still have to believe. I can't imagine what it's like to wake up every morning and doubt the value of the work you do.

Indeed, you need to love the work, and the industry, and yourself. I'm not ashamed to say that I'm a "realtophile." I love real estate agents. I really do, and I'm not just saying that because I happen to be one, and I'm a son to another, and a husband to another, and a brother to three more. I love them all. I love the agents who work with me, and I even love the agents who don't work with me (yet).

That's what we have to do for the Doubters—turn them from realtophobics who are afraid of the future to realtophiles who embrace it. Specifically, we need to show them that the real estate industry (1) does important work and (2) provides a valuable service (3) for a fair price. Let me explain.

1. The Work We Do

Over the last fifteen years, I've worked with thousands of real estate agents, and I see the dedication so many of them have to doing an important, difficult job in the face of often staggering obstacles.

I mean, what you do is really, really hard. If you're working with a buyer, you have to stay on top of a real estate inventory that changes every day. And you have to be able to read your buyer's needs, even when they're lying to you (or themselves) about what they truly want.

Then it's all the schlepping from house to house to house. Even when you find the right home, you have to see it a second time. Then a third time. And then, just to be sure, they have to see it with the whole family, including cousins, to get everyone's opinion.

Even if you get your buyers to make an offer, you still have to put together the transaction: negotiating the deal, counseling your buyer when they freak out about the inspection, dealing with the annoyances of attorneys or escrow agents, navigating the ridiculous mortgage process, counseling your buyer when they go berserk about a nail mark on a wall at the walkthrough, and then finally getting to a closing.

It's a staggering amount of work.

It's the same for listing agents working with a seller. You have to analyze the market, pull comps, and explain to the sellers that their home isn't quite worth as much as their neighbor, who is a dentist, told them. After that, you have to stage the home, which means finding a tactful way to explain to the sellers that, basically, they live like filthy animals.

Then you have to get the home on the market: taking pictures, writing descriptions, uploading the listing data, putting up a sign, and creating all your beautiful marketing materials. Then it's scheduling showings, chasing buyer agents for feedback, holding open houses, and staying in constant touch with sellers who won't be happy until you get them into contract.

Finally, even when you're successful getting them into contract, it's all the transactional work you need to keep that deal together: inspections, attorneys, escrow, mortgage, title, closing, and all the other stuff that you're accountable for without being responsible for.

Again, it's a staggering amount of work.

Not only that, but it's important work. We pay lip service to the concept, but buying a home really is the most important investment that most of our clients will ever make. And over the years, that investment has performed beautifully, making a lot of our clients very wealthy.

I know that some economists (and many Doubters) question the value of real estate investment over time, but they're wrong. Why? Because they always measure real estate as a "pure" financial investment, comparing it to stocks and bonds and all that. For example, they will usually compare someone buying a home versus someone investing in stock in, say, the 1970s. Then they'll simply measure the change of value over the last forty years. In those cases, real estate usually suffers by comparison as a pure appreciation play.

But when they're making their calculations, those economists always overlook something important—that guy who invested his money in the stock market rather than a house still has to live somewhere. Unless he's squatting in his parents' basement, he's paying rent. So if you're going to make a fair comparison, you have to factor in the unique nature of real estate investments: you can live in them. Even more than that, you have to consider some of the special advantages real estate provides: you can finance their purchase with a relatively small down payment, and you get tax advantages when you sell them.

Measured with all that in mind, real estate performs spectacularly. We all know people who got rich not because of the work they did for a living, but because of the investments they made. In 95 percent of those cases, they invested in real estate, not stocks.

Put it this way—I know lots of people who got seriously rich working on Wall Street, or investing in real estate; but I know a lot fewer people who got seriously rich investing in Wall Street, or (sadly) working in real estate.

2. The Market We Create

Agents should be proud of the way that they work together to create a thriving market for real estate in this country. Here's what I mean.

In economic theory, a market is just any place where buyers and sellers looking to transact goods and services can meet, where prices reflect the levels of supply and demand in the market. If demand goes up relative to supply, then the price will go up. If demand goes down relative to supply, the price will go down. We're all familiar with that dynamic, the foundation of basic economic theory.

So when economists talk about a "good" market, they mean a market that efficiently allows prices to reflect the true value of goods and services available—a market that is open, transparent, and fluid. That is, it has to be open to any willing participant, transparent in providing accurate information to buyers and sellers, and fluid enough to allow for easy transactions. If market participants don't have access, for example, to sound information about what comparable goods and services are selling for, or have sold for in the past, they cannot make truly efficient decisions about price.

That's what industry critics like the Disruptors and Discounters don't understand. They don't see how the real estate industry creates a beautifully efficient real estate market that provides buyers and sellers with openness, transparency, and fluidity.

Ask yourself this question: "What do homes in your local market sell for?" The answer: "Exactly what they are worth." Virtually every home in your market sells for its "true price"—what a group of buyers with full access to information about competing listings and comparable recent sales are willing to offer, and a seller with that same access is willing to accept.

Consider how the theoretical supply-and-demand principles play out in practice to ensure that homes sell for their true price. If a seller sets his price too high, his listing sits on the market until he reduces his price to the market price, at which point he'll start to get offers. If a seller sets his price too low, buyers will quickly inundate him with offers that will result in a "highest and best" bidding war that will likely drive the price back up to the market price.

Sellers can't overprice their homes because buyers know what other comparable homes have sold for and won't be tricked into overpaying. And buyers can't lowball sellers because in an open market someone will leap forward to outbid them.

But that market efficiency is only available because of the way that the real estate industry has adopted a cooperative multiple listing model in which all real estate agents put their inventory in a common market that incentivizes both the buyer and the seller side.

When an agent lists a home, she puts all the information about the home into the multiple listing marketplace, along with an offer of compensation designed to incentivize all the buyer agents to work to try to sell the home. That's what creates an open, transparent, and fluid market: the willingness of real estate brokers to cooperate with each other. And that cooperation is dependent on that offer of compensation that will provide a fair incentive to both sides of the transaction.

Think about it this way: shopping for a home is easier than shopping for a car. Yes, the actual transaction takes longer, but that's mostly because of the relative complexity of the financing. But the shopping experience itself, which is what we have control over, is much easier.

Let's say, for example, that you were looking to buy an upscale sedan. You do your research and find that about a dozen different carmakers have vehicles in your price range. But you can't buy a car without seeing it in person, so you have to visit each dealer. You can't just go to one dealer and see all the cars on the market. Indeed, if you have two Cadillac dealers in your area, you have to go to both of them. Why? Because the dealers don't cooperate. They don't share inventory in a pool.

Moreover, you have to go through your whole shopping experience without any help. Everyone you meet at the dealership works for the seller, not for you. You don't get any help setting up visits or test drives, and you don't get anyone who can advise you on recent sales or counsel you on your offer. You're on your own.

(I've always wondered, in fact, whether someone could start a successful business offering buyer agency to car buyers. You hire a car agent, and you get someone who knows everything about any car on the market, helps you narrow your preferences, takes you on showings, negotiates for you, and helps you through the transactional process. Wouldn't that be a better experience? I think a lot of people, particularly those who get spooked by the car-buying process, would be willing to pay a few hundred dollars (and get their car insurance) for that kind of service. Feel free to steal the idea. I'm pretty busy, but I'll be happy to invest.)

Shopping for a home is an easier experience. All the brokers pool their listings into a common inventory so you can work with any member agent and get access to anything that's for sale. You can access sales records that tell you what comparable homes have sold for and to get an idea of what kinds of offers you can make. Most importantly, you get an agent who is on your side, helping you sift through the inventory and counseling you throughout the process.

Real estate is just a much more efficient market: it's fluid, transparent, and open. But that efficiency is only available because agents don't hoard their listings the way that car dealers maintain their own exclusive inventory, and because buyer agents are incentivized to provide services that give buyers a better and more transparent experience. Without the incentives provided by a two-sided deal, the real estate market would look at lot more like the car-buying market.

And no one wants that. Except, of course, the Disruptors who are trying to displace the market, and the Discounters who are trying to starve out the two-sided deal.

3. The Fees We Charge

For all that service, people still complain about how much real estate agents make. Sellers carp that commissions are too high; buyers demand a rebate; and Disruptors and Discounters malign us as middlemen who extract a fee for inserting ourselves into the transaction.

I once had to go into court when our sellers refused to pay the contracted fee, simply on the ground that it was too high. Now, it was true that the clients had agreed to a commission that was at the very high end of what was customarily offered by sellers in our market. But at the time they entered the listing, the clients were in a huge rush and under enormous pressure to sell the home quickly. They believed that offering a larger commission would accelerate the sale. They were correct: the home went into contract in about two weeks in a relatively weak market.

Sadly, when we went in front of the judge to explain the situation, the judge sided with the sellers, agreeing that the higher commission wasn't justified, regardless of what the contract said. Why? Because we had done the job too well! Here's what the judge said: "Well, if the property sold so quickly, you didn't have to work so hard to sell it." Of course, if the listing had taken two years to sell, and we went to court to collect more because of all the extra work we had to do, I'm certain we would have been laughed out of court. And I don't remember any sellers ever agreeing to pay us any part of our fee when their home didn't sell, simply because we worked so hard on it.

That's the kind of environment we face. If we don't sell the home, we didn't do our job, and we don't get paid. But if we sell the home quickly, we didn't work hard enough, we don't deserve our full compensation. Imagine cutting a doctor's bill because she healed you too quickly.

But it's bad enough if other people think that way. We can't afford to think that way. We have to believe that we're worth it, or we're doomed.

Here's the best way to think about challenges to our fee model. If someone is going to complain that real estate agents are overpaid, challenge them to answer this question: *Overpaid compared to whom?* (Use *whom*, by the way, not *who*. It's not only technically correct, but it also sounds classy!)

Here's what I mean. If people are going to say that we're over-paid, then they have to provide a fair point for comparison. And they need to make that comparison to a professional providing a similar type of service to real estate brokerage.

Let's assume for the moment that a real estate broker charges a 6 percent contingency commission if the home sells, stipulating of course for the good people at the Justice Department that all real estate commissions are negotiable, because I am far too pretty to go to jail. Now, we all know that this 6 percent gets split in some way between two agents: the seller's agent and the buyer's agent. So let's just assume that they each get 3 percent.

Is a 3 percent fee for helping someone sell a home, or buy a home, out of line, given all the work that has to be done? Let's compare that 6 percent fee to what other professionals charge for similar types of work:

- *Personal Injury Attorneys.* If you broke your leg in a slip-and-fall accident in a supermarket, you would probably hire a personal injury attorney to represent you in a civil action to recover compensation for your injuries. Most likely, that attorney would charge you a contingency fee of about 30 to 35 percent of your recovery, plus expenses. Your lawyer ends up making about a third of what you recover, and she still has two working legs.

- *Financial Planners.* If you had some serious money to invest in the markets, you might hire a financial planner to manage it for you. What do they make? Usually, they collect a small percentage of the amount you invest, maybe 1 percent or so. So that's lower than the average real estate commission. But here's the key: they charge it every year. That's not 1 percent when you invest the money; it's 1 percent over and over again for as long as you maintain the investment. Indeed, some money managers also get a percentage of your appreciation (of course, they don't share in your losses).

- *Interior Decorators.* Your buyer purchases a home from you and decides she wants to redecorate everything. So she hires an interior decorator. What's the fee? The standard charge for interior design is an hourly consultation rate, usually a few hundred dollars per hour. That's pretty good, right? Well, on top of that, the decorator often gets a 30 to 35 percent commission on everything you buy. That's supposed to reflect the savings that you get from buying at the "decorator discount price," but how are they savings if you don't actually get to save them?

Compared to those compensation systems, the fees charged by real estate brokers seem reasonable. That 35 percent attorney contingency fee sounds nice to me, and I certainly would be amenable to giving up a transactional commission in exchange for a yearly fee to manage my client's real estate portfolio.

Now, some might balk at those comparisons, pointing out that attorneys and financial planners generally have more education and professional training than real estate agents. That's a fair point, but what about interior decorators? They don't need college degrees. They work on improving home value. Yet they get a reasonable hourly rate, plus a commission on everything you purchase.

Indeed, it's not just interior decorators—most service professionals charge an hourly rate rather than a fee based on a successful outcome, a compensation model that I daresay most real estate agents would be happy to adopt. Think about how nice it would be to get paid by the hour for representing buyers and sellers. You would just agree to your rate with the client in advance and get paid for all that time you had to spend schlepping them around the county or moving their furniture around to create feng shui. I think most of us would take that deal.

But most of our clients wouldn't. Buyers like the fact that they don't have to pay out-of-pocket for all the services they get from a real estate agent. Most of them never think about the fact that although the seller pays the commission, it's actually built into the price of the home. Indeed, most buyers would rather pay the fee through the purchase price, which allows them to finance it over the long term of their loan.

Even though sellers are the ones who complain about commission rates, few of them would be willing to pay an agent by the hour. After all, one of the sweet features of the typical real estate commission is that it's contingent on the sale, so agents only get paid if they're successful in selling the home.

What if we make the comparison to the other professionals just in the real estate transaction? Is our hypothetical 3 percent broker-age fee per side reasonable compared to the customary charges of mortgage lenders, inspection engineers, title agents, closing attorneys, and professional stagers? Those fees can vary a lot depending on where you are in the country, so forgive me if I make the comparison point to my home state of New York:

- *Mortgage lenders.* Most lenders gross about 1.5 percent to 3 percent on the size of their buyers' loans, which is roughly comparable to what real estate brokers earn from representing those same buyers. Now, I love loan officers as much as I love real estate agents, so I'm not calling them overpaid, but I think even they would agree that buyer agents spend more time putting together a deal than loan officers spend in securing a mortgage.

- *Title fees.* Title insurance fees in New York are set by state law, so you can't discount them, and they range based on the price of the home. But, as a rough estimate, title insurance costs about 1 percent of the price of the home, and title agents keep about 80 percent of that. So that's significantly less than what real estate brokers charge. But the work isn't really comparable. Most title reports take a few hours to produce, and title agents pass through many of their production expenses. On an hour-by-hour comparison, title agents are paid much more than real estate agents (at least in New York).

- *Inspections.* Inspection engineers in my market make about $400 to $500 for an inspection report that takes several hours to prepare. Maybe they average $75 to $100 per hour, an hourly rate that is probably a lot higher than what real estate agents collect on most of their deals.

- *Closing attorneys.* Most states outside the Northeast don't require attorneys to close real estate transactions. But in my area, real estate attorneys charge anywhere from $750 to $2,000 to represent a client for a transaction, which is good compensation for what is usually just a few hours of work to revise or review a standard contract, have a few meetings or calls with the clients, review title work, and perform a closing. They make less than real estate agents on a deal, but they also generally have to do a lot less work. Again, if you broke it down to an hourly rate, I think that attorneys would come out ahead.

Again, my point is not to say that any of these professionals are overpaid. They're not. But we need to understand that real estate brokerage fees are fairly reasonable given the amount of work that the average real estate agent has to do to procure and close a sale.

So if people ever challenge your fee, ask them, "Overpaid compared to whom?" Rather than get flustered and feel like you have to justify your value, put them on the defensive and make them back it up.

Doubters need to pick up their heads. This is a great industry. At our best, we provide a terrific service that clients need for a fair price. Moreover, panic is not going to help fight off the challenges posed by Disruptors and Discounters. If we just run around like Chicken Little, or hide our head in the ground like an ostrich, we're going to bring about the future we're trying to avoid.

If you need some external validation to make you feel better, then think about this: Warren Buffett is the greatest investor in history. His company, Berkshire Hathaway, is buying real estate brokerages. He knows better than you. He's no Doubter.

Conclusion: Stop Giving Permission

FABLED ADVICE COLUMNIST ANN LANDERS used to get letters from people spinning a tale of woe about how someone was taking advantage of them. Maybe an aunt was staying with them well past the expiration date on what was supposed to be a short visit. Maybe a neighbor was constantly borrowing and not returning tools. Maybe a friend was always coming up short when the lunch check dropped on the table. Complaints like that.

Here's what she used to say: "No one can take advantage of you without your permission."

In other words, your aunt is still staying in your guest room because you're letting her. Your neighbor has half your tool set because you won't stop him. And your friend is getting subsidized meals because you're still picking up the tab. So stop giving your permission.

I would say the same thing about the threats we face as an industry: no one can disrupt our industry without our permission. We've done this to ourselves.

We did this by thinking about ourselves, not about the people who pay us—our clients.

We did this to ourselves by often hiring the wrong people, training them poorly, and giving them little support in how to do their job well.

We did this to ourselves by failing to adapt our value proposition as our clients' needs changed.

We did this to ourselves by focusing all our innovative energies on how to generate leads, rather than improving the real estate transaction.

And we did this to ourselves by losing faith in ourselves and in what we do.

Ultimately, we've given permission to these Disruptors and Discounters and fueled the anxieties of the Doubters, by losing our focus. We oriented the business to our needs, rather than to our clients and their needs.

But it's not too late to change. We can do this. We can adapt our value proposition right now. We can change the way that we think about our clients' needs and about how to service those needs. And we can take back control of our business.

No one can take our industry without our permission. So let's stop giving it.

Afterword: Three Keys to Change for All My Industry Friends

I WROTE THIS BOOK FOR THE REAL ESTATE INDUSTRY. What's the industry? As I said in the Introduction, it obviously includes real estate brokers and agents, numerically the largest groups of people who make up the industry. But I also think that the industry includes anyone else who supports brokers and agents in helping people buy and sell real estate:

- Franchise systems and independent networks that align different groups of brokers and agents together

- The training industry, not just the major players like Tom Ferry and Brian Buffini, but anyone who coaches or trains agents in venues large and small

- Partners, also called vendors, who provide technology, systems, or other support for the rest of us

Because I am writing for the larger audience, I didn't really have a chance to drill down for ideas relevant for each of those industry players individually. So I've put together this Afterword simply to articulate three changes that I would suggest for each group.

All that said, a note of clarification. Throughout this book, I've often referred to practices that we did at my brokerage, usually things that worked out. I didn't tell you about the failures, even though they're also instructive, because I am deeply ashamed by all of them. But we had a lot of them too.

So by making all these suggestions, I don't mean to imply that my brokerage is perfect, or that we ourselves have made all the changes that I suggest in this book. If anything, this book represents an idealized vision of what this industry should be, and I think that as long as I'm working toward realizing that vision, I'm probably going in the right direction. The destination is important, but so is the journey.

Agents

Agents are on the front lines working with buyers and sellers every day, which makes them the ones most impacted by the disruption and dislocation potentially coming to the industry. So most of this book is already directed at them: stop thinking like (just) a salesperson, focus on client needs, modernize your value proposition, believe in yourself, and so on. Moreover, at the risk of indulgent self-promotion, I've written another book entitled *How to Be a Great Real Estate Agent*, which might be out by the time you read this, and which gives many more pages of advice for how agents can thrive today.

But if I were to try to distill all those pages into a three-suggestion summary for how agents themselves can change in the client-centric era, it would be these:

1. **Generate business by satisfying client needs.** Traditional lead generation is always focused on the agent and her needs—her need for a buyer, a listing, a deal, money. But a better way to develop your business is to focus on what other people need, and how you can satisfy them, even when you're engaging in traditional prospecting methodologies. For example, if you're trying to get an appointment with a for-sale-by-owner, why not think about what he might need if he's trying to sell his house on his own? Maybe a CMA, or guidelines for running his own open house, or references for attorneys, for example. The idea is that instead of just approaching him to find out when he plans on hiring an agent, go to him with something of value that might help you build a relationship. You can do that for any type of lead generation: find out what that person needs and approach them by servicing the need rather than running some ancient script on them.

2. **Give consultations, not presentations.** On behalf of the real estate training industry, I want to apologize to you for teaching you how to do listing presentations all wrong. For some ungodly reason, we taught you that you should go in and put on a show. Who else does

that? Guys who sell cheap blinds, that's who. Most other professionals, when they meet a client or customer for the first time, don't start by talking about themselves. Rather, they start by asking questions, which not only starts to build rapport and trust, but also helps them determine what that client or customer needs from them. And it's a lot easier than delivering some canned presentation with memorized scripts. So stop thinking about that initial meeting as an audition for the job, and just do the job—find out what the client needs and start giving it to her.

3. Be great at your job. Most importantly, learn how to be great at your job. Know your market. Know your inventory. Know how to manage transactions. You need to know how to do all those CORE services I outlined as part of the value proposition. So study and learn and grow. On top of all that, spend some time learning about great client service as a discipline of its own: what makes great service and how to ensure you're providing it consistently and effectively.

Brokers

Brokers, I get it. I'm one of you. I know how hard it is to run a profitable business with splits going up, expenses going up, and commission rates going down. The key is that you have to focus on what's important. I think of brokerage revenue as going into three buckets: (1) the agents, which is by far the biggest bucket; (2) expenses, the second biggest; and (3) profit, which is comparatively more like a thimble.

The goal of running a brokerage is to put as much in that first bucket as you need to keep agents happy and motivated, and then as much in that third bucket so you can make a living. That leaves the second bucket. Your mission is to shrink that second bucket as much as you can, so you can put more in your agents', and your own, pocket. So if I had to pull out three guidelines for shrinking that bucket, it would be these.

1. Only pay for things your agents value, unless they're wrong. If you're paying for something that your agents don't value, then you should probably get rid of it, because that allows you to pay them more (which keeps them happy and around) or pay yourself more (which gives you a reason to get up every day). You'll be amazed at all the expenses that you can eliminate without them caring, if they understand that the savings is mostly going to them. For example, we discovered after the crash, when like many of you we were forced to cut expenses, that agents didn't value a personal assistant program we'd been running. Why? Because technology had mostly rendered it obsolete, and agents could easily do for themselves tasks that they used to need an assistant for. So we cut it, gave some to the agents, and a little bit to ourselves. Everyone wins. One caveat: don't get rid of it if they're wrong. Meaning, don't get rid of something they don't value if you truly think it's necessary. But if you think they're wrong, you better be right.

2. Stop thinking like a retail business. The same way that agents need to stop thinking like salespeople, brokers need to stop thinking like we're in the retail business. It's killing us. We end up with all this expensive space in the middle of Main Street in every small village and town in our market. No parking. No good conference space. Agents fighting over desks. Why are you there? Because five years ago you had a rental walk-in? Please. Real estate is not an impulse purchase. You don't need to be in a retail space. Go get cheaper space in an office park somewhere, which has parking and conference rooms and all that. And move toward regional offices that cover all those little towns and villages. Law firms have one office that services a region; why shouldn't brokerages? If we're going to limit our expenses so we can put more in the agent and profit buckets, facility costs is the first thing that has to go.

3. Systematize your operation. As you try to shrink that expense bucket, keep in mind that systems are generally a lot cheaper than people. If you create good systems, you can run your company with fewer people. So every brokerage should have an operational manual that articulates best practices for running each office. For example, I'm a big fan of checklists. If I come up with a good checklist that sets out what every administrator and manager should do in a given situation, I don't need a genius to follow it. Geniuses are expensive. Non-geniuses are cheaper.

Franchises and Other Networks

I have a soft spot for franchises. My company has been with a franchise since its inception in the early 1980s—Century 21, then Prudential, and now Better Homes and Gardens Real Estate. And though we've gotten a lot out of each of those franchise relationships, I realize it's not for everyone, and you have to do what works for you. But even brokers who are independent are often a member of a network of some kind that supplies them with some franchise-like value, like Leading Real Estate Companies of the World or the Realty Alliance. And almost all of us are members of the largest network of all, the National Association of REALTORS.

These networks, particularly franchises, are changing, and they have to change. Traditionally, real estate franchise systems took that "each office independently owned and operated" language that they put in every ad very seriously. They provided mostly marketing tools, a brand name, some back-end systems, and otherwise left brokers to their own devices. It wasn't like running a McDonald's, where you buy a franchise, go to their hamburger school, and then do things the way they tell you to do them.

Franchises traditionally never provided brokers with a blueprint for how to manage their business: how to structure splits, allocate expenses, train and manage agents, identify locations, and so on. In real estate franchises, we generally got to cook the burgers however we wanted, so long as we paid our fees.

But that seems to be changing, maybe because the growth of Keller Williams showed other franchise systems how a strong, structured format could make it easier to quickly build franchisees. So now I'm seeing even Realogy, which has always taken a hands-off approach to telling franchisees how to run their business and was rigidly disciplined about keeping a separation among the brands, building centralized systems to provide higher-level services to its franchisees. We get a lot more of our systems, for example, from Better Homes and Gardens Real Estate (part of Realogy) than we did from Prudential, which I think is at least partly a reflection of how franchises have changed in the ten years since we changed affiliations.

So my three suggestions for franchises (and by extension those other networks) would all be about advancing more toward that format franchise model:

1. **Help brokers implement best practices.** Brokers are getting squeezed on both ends—splits and expenses go up, commission rates go down. They need help finding ways to become more efficient and

effective. Luckily, these industry networks (franchises, Leading RE, NAR, and others) are in a perfect position to identify best practices for managing profitable brokerages and articulate them for their members. For example, Realogy and Home Services both run their own huge independently operated brokerages on a very high level, so they must be constantly identifying best practice efficiencies that they could propagate throughout the affiliated franchise networks. And other industry associations have a lot of shared data that they could learn from. They know how best to cook the burgers, while we're still making it up as we go along. They could help us be better.

2. Carve out a consumer identity. As I wrote in the value proposition chapter, too many real estate brands have become commodified from a consumer's perspective. They all stand for "we sell real estate," but most of them don't say much about the way they sell real estate. The only exceptions prove the rule, since Sotheby's, Better Homes and Gardens Real Estate, and Berkshire Hathaway trade on their associations with iconic brands, rather than build a brand on their own. Similarly, we know in the industry that RE/MAX and Keller Williams are different from other franchises, but that's because of their internal agent-centric business model, not their client-centric consumer appeal. This is not easy, obviously, but if I ran a franchise, I'd want to find a way to carve out my own place in this industry, and rather than be all things to all people, I'd be everything to some people.

3. Make conferences about something. This might seem like a minor point, but we could do a better job with our conferences. All of us. We're still following the same format we did twenty-five years ago: general sessions in the morning with keynote speakers, usually some sort of celebrity who gives a generic talk, and then breakouts in the afternoon with a million ninety-minute shallow dives, usually teasers from trainers of what you could get if you bought their system or promotional talks about franchise systems and programs. I think that's a mistake. Brad Inman gets as many people to each of his twice-yearly conferences as any of the large brands because he makes his conference about something. Tom Ferry and Brian Buffini get huge crowds to their retreats because they make them about something. They don't do deep dives, and people come away feeling like they were inspired to make changes in their lives. Every conference should be like that. I don't want to hear Larry King talk about Yogi Berra again. Give me something I can use.

The Training Industry

I think I sometimes come across as critical of the real estate educational industry. If that's true, it's only because I see myself as part of that industry, and I'm incredibly self-critical. I think we could all be doing better.

But just to be clear, I love and respect all these people who have made their careers helping agents become successful. I first heard Mike Ferry speak when I was eighteen, and I can still remember some of the lessons about self-motivation. Floyd Wickman is the best I've ever seen at building persuasive dialogues, a master craftsman of the English language. Danielle Kennedy taught me things about farming that I never heard anywhere else. Brian Buffini took a deceptively simple concept about personal relationship building and turned it into one of the most powerful coaching programs in the industry. Tom Ferry is simply brilliant, the most well-rounded trainer working today, and a master motivator.

I learned from all of them. They're all great. They all deserve to be in whatever hall of fame we create for the real estate training industry. If I disagree with them about certain things, that doesn't diminish the immense respect I have for them, or my gratitude for how they've helped me understand this business. The same goes for all the other talented coaches working today, including Larry Kendall, Verl Workman, Dan Allen, Darryl Davis, Leigh Brown, Alyssa Hellman, and many, many more.

It's not just about them. It's about all the hard-working company trainers at individual brokerages, franchise systems, and networks, helping their agents learn the business. It's about the indefatigable educators training at the local boards and associations, or working the conference circuit, and touching thousands of agents every year. They all command my deepest respect.

So it is with that deep appreciation that I make these suggestions:

1. Teach service as much as sales. Obviously, I took a strong position in this book about changing the training emphasis in this industry. We focus too much on developing sales skills, and not enough on helping agents do their jobs. When we do try to teach substantive skills, we tend to make it more about regulatory and ethical compliance than about being great at our jobs. We could be doing this better. And we certainly need to start teaching customer service as its own discipline.

2. Have a point of view. If you were to pull out the training programs provided by most big brokers, franchise systems, or real estate boards, you'd find that they're basically the same. They're all filled with tried-and-true conventional wisdom about how agents should build their business: here's how to build your sphere, here's how to give a listing presentation, here's how to call a FSBO—and on and on. But if you were to see a national trainer, you'd find major differences in the way they teach. There's no way you'd mistake, for example, a Mike Ferry seminar for a Brian Buffini conference. Why? Because sales coaches have a distinct point of view, because they came up with their program on their own. They didn't hire a committee to write it for them. But, too often, institutional players like franchises, big brokers, and boards build their programs by committee, which eliminates any possibility of establishing a distinct point of view. That's why agents will pay a lot of money to hear a national trainer and never crack open that free training manual they get from their broker or franchisor.

3. Integrate with systems. I can remember going to see Brian years ago, and someone asking him what CRM they should use. Now, a database system is absolutely essential for running Brian's referral system, yet he didn't have a CRM he recommended. I thought it was a real gap in his value package. Since then, to his great credit, he's filled that gap, building a nifty app called Referral Maker that is the perfect articulation of his system. Tom does the same thing, constantly recommending the technology tools that you need to implement his systems. All of us trainers need to do that. We're long past the point when you could teach people what to do without showing them how to do it. If you want them to make listing videos, you have to show them how to use the technology they'll need to put them online. If you want them to work a farm, you need to recommend the mailing program. Otherwise, you're just giving people empty calories.

Partners

We shouldn't call them vendors anymore. The implication that they're outside the industry isn't really accurate. Tech companies like First.io, Spacio, OpCity, CallAction, CE Shop, and all the rest—they're as much as part of the industry as everyone else. They supply the technology and tools that power brokers and agents to service clients, so we want to enlist them in helping us avoid disruption as well. Even the often-maligned Zillow, which some Doubters think of as a Disruptor, has been an indispensable ally for many agents and brokers in building their business.

So what should these partners be doing to help us get better as an industry?

1. **Be great at one thing, and integrate with the rest.** Until a few years ago, my company developed most of the technologies that the agents used. Our platform was pretty good, customized to our systems and training philosophy and comprehensive: everything from CRM to presentation software to market analysis systems. It was really quite good, but over time it became tougher and tougher to keep up. So when we went looking for a replacement, we first tried to find a partner who had built something similarly comprehensive, but we couldn't find anything that replicated that seamless experience that we'd built in-house. In the end, we went entirely the other way, stitching together the best programs we found to provide each service independently, connected only through our extranet and API keys. And it worked because we got what we thought was the "best in show" for CRM, CMA, marketing, market analysis, and the rest with companies like MoxiWorks, Imprev, ListTrac, and Collateral Analytics. That's what I would recommend to the partners out there—be the best at what you do and be nimble enough to integrate with any other systems out there. Don't try to do everything.

2. **Empower agents to be better at their jobs.** I can understand why so many tech partners are chasing after the same rabbit—how to generate and convert more leads. It makes sense because that's what agents and brokers obsess over and what they're willing to pay for. Over the last few years, though, we've started to see more start-ups who are trying to improve the client-service experience: Updater, RealScout, Aventree, RealSatisfied, among others. The extent to

which companies are still trying to generate business, they're focusing not just on conversion of low-yield, "find out more" website leads, but on, for example, First.io's predictive analytic technology that allows agents to focus their attention on building relationships with people who are statistically more likely to need their services. Help agents build relationships with the people they know, not follow up on anonymous leads.

3. **Focus on helping agents do better what they're already doing.** In my experience, the best tech partners find ways to make agents better at what they're already doing, rather than giving them something new to do. For example, Spacio provides agents with a better way of doing something they were already doing: signing people into open houses and following up with them. ShowingTime provides agents with a better way of setting appointments. SmartZip helps agents improve their marketing by focusing on people who are most likely to move. In contrast, too many tech companies want to get agents (or consumers, for that matter) to do something they're not already doing. Like all those blog platforms from ten years ago that failed miserably. Why? Because agents weren't writers, and trying to get them to write was forcing them to do something new.

Also, in the section on improving the transaction, I talked about how we absolutely need a universal transaction communication platform that integrates API feeds from all the major players in a real estate deal: agents, inspection, mortgage, title, escrow, attorney, insurance, and anyone else who provides services to the client. Would someone please build that? Thanks!

Multiple Listing Systems

Full disclosure: when it comes to multiple listing systems, I've always been a "don't level the playing field kind of guy." After all, I own a big brokerage, one of the largest in that association. And like a lot of big brokers, I don't really want the MLS to take dues money, a good percentage of which comes from agents within my company, and use it to invest in tools, programs, or services that replicate what I offer as a broker, eliminating an advantage I might have over the lower-service brokers that compete with me. That's never made sense to me, or a lot of other big brokers.

Now, I recognize my own bias in this discussion, and understand that a lot of brokers and agents favor more ambitious MLS systems that provide public-facing websites and robust agent-centric technology and all that. That's fine, reasonable people can disagree about that sort of thing. But we should at least acknowledge the tension in asking the MLS to play a role in helping the real estate industry rise above the challenges of disruption: namely, some brokers and agents don't want the MLS to do anything new at all.

So if we're going to encourage the MLS to be a part of the solution, we should focus on initiatives that align with what the MLS is already doing, and are less likely to alarm the "don't level the playing field" types (like me). Specifically, I would suggest that MLS systems build off their core competencies of facilitating standardization and collaboration among brokers and agents, particularly in situations where the MLS wouldn't be neutralizing any perceived competitive advantage for individual brokers or agents.

For example, the MLS provides the common platform for offers of cooperation among brokers, which is the grease for the gears of the transparent real estate market. And the MLS standardizes the sharing of listing information among participants, which is what allows them all to disseminate inventory across the internet. Those are vital services, but only a common carrier like the MLS could provide them – no broker could unilaterally announce or enforce those types of standards.

So if I had to identify three suggestions for how MLS systems can play a role in improving the industry, I'd focus on ideas that would align with those core services:

1. **Develop more transactional collaboration platforms.** The MLS should find new and creative ways to help brokers and agents collaborate when they're putting together transactions. We have a lot of chaos in the real estate transaction that could be reduced with better collaboration tools across brokerages. In most markets, for example, agents don't have a uniform way to make offers. They send offers by email, or text, or phone, or on non-standardized offer sheets that are scanned (or even faxed!) and have different ways to present terms. And few jurisdictions have firm rules on how to handle multiple offer situations, which creates a tremendous flash point in hot

markets, where buyer-side agents often feel abused and mistreated when their offers are not accepted.

So why can't an MLS step in to implement some sort of standardized, cooperative platform for presenting offers, one that would make it easy to make, receive, or compare offers from any agent or broker in the system? No brokers have a "competitive advantage" in how they write offers, so you're not running into trouble there. And the whole system of presenting and negotiating offers would be so much easier if everyone had a common platform to work with.

But that's just one example—a creative MLS could find all sorts of ways to facilitate more efficient cooperation among its members, without alarming the "don't level the playing field" crowd. Transaction communication, scheduling showings, providing and receiving showing feedback, e-signatures – anytime you have a dynamic that by its nature involves agents from different brokerages, you have an opportunity for the MLS to create a standard system that makes the interaction more efficient for everyone.

2. Develop buyer-side services that mirror what we provide to sellers. One of the best services the MLS provides is the standardized processing of home sellers. Most home sellers have to sign a contract approved by the MLS. Then, they have to submit their listing information, though their agent and broker, into an MLS-provided intake system. And then their listing information is distributed to the rest of the MLS members. All very standardized.

But what about buyers? Most MLS systems govern every aspect of a broker's relationship with a seller (i.e., the listing), but do nothing to facilitate or manage the relationship with a buyer. Why is that? Probably because, even today, most agents in most markets don't get buyers to sign representation agreements. They won't work with a seller without an exclusive right to sell contract, but they'll work with a buyer on a handshake (or less).

The MLS could help remedy that, creating a standardized way for an agent and broker to formalize their relationship with a buyer. Just take the system we use for sellers, and flip it for buyers. Sign a representation agreement, submit it to MLS, and "register" that buyer (anonymously) to that agent for the term of the agreement – enforceable against other agents the same way that a listing agreement is. Then disseminate that aggregated buyer information to all member participants, to create a "buyer inventory" that could engender all sorts of creative opportunities for smart brokers, agents, and partners.

Buyers and sellers are both consumers of real estate services. Why should they be treated differently?

3. Provide competency education. Finally, MLS systems have a unique advantage over all the other major players in the industry in taking ownership of competency education: namely, the MLS doesn't get paid on the transaction, and isn't wedded to the outcome of any particular real estate deal. Brokers, agents, franchisors – their fortunes are all tied to the revenue generated from a transaction. Most trainers and tech partners make money if they can help agents generate deals.

But MLS systems are different. Yes, they generally benefit if their members do well, but they don't get paid on a particular closing. This puts them in a unique position to offer robust competency education – training that helps agents learn the fundamentals about how to be good at their jobs. Agents don't get that kind of education in licensing, and they generally don't get it from their brokers – so why would brokers, even the "playing field" ones, complain if the MLS filled that gap? After all, if I know that my agents are learning fundamentals from the MLS, I can focus my training on taking them to the next level.

More importantly, competency training aligns with the MLS role of facilitating collaboration. All of us know the pain of trying to do a deal with some hapless agent who doesn't know what he's doing. Setting up a basic foundational level of competence would benefit all the members, to the disadvantage of none.

Let's Get to Work

This book is just the beginning of this conversation. We can continue the discussion at JoeRand.com where you'll find my industry blog and my latest thoughts on these issues. Of course, you can buy my other books, if they're out yet. If you liked this book, you'll probably like them. But like them or not, you should buy them. Many copies.

Oh, and if you know anyone who wants to buy or sell in New York City's northern suburbs, give me a call and I'll put them in touch with one of my great agents.

Let's get to work.

Acknowledgments

I WROTE THIS BOOK BECAUSE I MISSED A FLIGHT.

Seriously. In April 2017, I was all set to go to a conference in Denver. Bags packed. In the car. Three hours to get to the airport. All good!

Unfortunately, I made the mistake of booking a morning flight out of LaGuardia when apparently everyone in the tri-state area was making their morning commute. Then I had the bad luck of hitting a terrible rainstorm that made every driver cautiously slow. And then I was ultimately stymied because I stupidly assumed that Gate 3c was in Terminal C. LaGuardia is a terrible place. Never fly out of LaGuardia.

So I missed my flight, and all the other flights to Denver were booked solid.

Dejected, wet, and stressed from three hours of stop-and-go driving, I trudged back to my car, ready to head to the office for just another routine day of work.

And then I realized: everyone thought I was in Denver. I had said my goodbyes to my kids. I had put an away message on my voice-mail. I had set an auto-responder on my email. No one expected me in the office for another three days. I was free!

Smarter people probably would have gotten on the next flight to somewhere in the Caribbean.

But I decided to write. I went to my empty summer home on the Jersey Shore and started the book I'd been trying to write for three years. No phone calls. No emails. No one coming in with problems to dump on my desk. Just writing.

Three days later, I had finished half a book. Then about 150 days later, writing early in the morning before anyone else got to the office, I finished the other half.

So I guess the first person I should thank is Steve Murray, whose Gathering of Eagles conference in Denver is the one I missed. Sorry about that, Steve, but thanks for your inadvertent and involuntary contribution to this book.

But I have a lot of other people I need to thank as well, whose contributions went far beyond scheduling a conference that I missed:

First, to my partners in the Rand family business—Marsha, Greg, Matt, and Dan—who have been the best partners I could have ever asked for, and who supported me unconditionally through my long creative process, most of which involved my pacing around our offices accomplishing little.

To my friends and colleagues at the Rand real estate company, especially all our wonderful agents, who over the years patiently endured my infliction of unconventional ideas, the best of which ultimately made it into this book; the worst of which are hopefully long forgotten and never to be mentioned again.

In particular, my thanks to all the great people in our leadership team, past and present, who make my life easier every day, including Paul Adler, Rosemarie Glasel, Marc Catuogno, June Stokes, Arlyne Ashkinos, Barbara Meyer, Renee Zurlo, Denise Friend, Justin Wrobel, Chris Rand, James Coombs, J. P. Endres, Roberta Bangs, Mabel Gutierrez, Yvonne Regan, Janet Farsetta, Jamie Troia, Lindsay Newler, and my righthand man Adam DiFrancesco.

To Better Homes and Gardens Real Estate CEO Sherry Chris, who has been my model for industry activism and an unstinting partner to the Rand family company. And in that same vein, to former Realogy CEO Alex Perriello and Chairman Richard A. Smith for their unwavering and generous support of me and my family, and to Realogy's incoming leadership, Ryan M. Schneider and John Peyton.

To the tireless educators in the real estate industry, both national and in my local area, who inspire and challenge me to this day, including Tom Ferry, Mike Ferry, Brian Buffini, Floyd Wickman, Larry Kendall, Darryl Davis, Mark Leader, Bernice Ross, Alyssa Hellman, Leigh Brown, Jeff Lobb, Katie Lance, Valerie Garcia, Amy Chorew,

Roseann Farrow, Lisa Aaron, Priscilla Toth, Sean Carpenter, and too many others to name in the space I have.

To all the brilliant industry people who have bounced ideas with me over the years, or galvanized me with their own vision, including Victor Lund, Marc Davison, Brian Boero, Joel Burslem, Steve Murray, Stefan Swanepoel, Pam O'Connor, Andrew Flachner, Laura Monroe, Gregg Borodaty, Melissa Kwan, Nicolai Kolding, Jennifer Marchetti, Vanessa Jones Bergmark, York Bauer, Katie Maxwell, Michael Sklarz, Norman Miller, Mark Choey, John VanDerWall, Andrew Downs, Ginger Wilcox, Alex Lange, Phil Faranda, Mike Schneider, Seth Price, Nicole Beauchamp, Greg Schwartz, Leslie Ebersole, Billy Ekofo, Audie Chamberlain, Kendyl Young, Jonathan Aizen, Eddie Berenbaum, Ben Kinney, Jay Thompson, Kevin Levent, Craig McClelland, Jennifer Hawkins, Denee Evans, Shelley Specchio, Nick Segal, Austin Allison, Jeff Turner, David Friedman, and, of course, never (again) to be forgotten, the Notorious R.O.B. himself, Rob Hahn.

To Craig Cheatham and all my much, much smarter colleagues at the Realty Alliance, who set the tone for this industry.

To Brad Inman, who challenged me to find my voice, and then raise my voice.

To John Featherston, a great friend to my family, who always gave me a podium.

To Julie Trelstad and her amazing team, who made this book a reality, and to Lois Kroplick, who made it a possibility.

Most importantly, to my wife, Linie, and my kids, Jake and Relly, for making any of it worthwhile.

And, finally, to LaGuardia Airport for being so very, very terrible.

Excerpt

From Joe Rand's Next Book, **How to be a Great Real Estate Agent: The Principles and Practice of Client-Oriented Real Estate**

Available November 2018

Let's start with some simple questions.

Who's your accountant?

If I met you at a cocktail party and told you I needed an accountant help me pay my taxes, do you have a name that you'd give me? Okay, great! Because the government appreciates your financial support.

Who's your dentist?

You do have a dentist, right? I mean, I hope you do. If you don't, you should probably just put the book down right now and go find yourself a dentist, because that's just not healthy. Seriously. Go right now. We'll wait. Your health comes first.

Who's your hair stylist?

I've asked that question to a lot of audiences, and I generally find that most men can't give me a name, because many of them are bald, and most of the rest are filthy animals that don't care how they look. But women – they almost always have a hair stylist, usually someone they've gone to for a long time. So they have a name.

Okay, so here's where we stand: you've told me that you have an accountant, and a dentist, and maybe a hair stylist.

Now, just one more question:

How many people would say that you're their real estate agent?

Think about it. If I came to your town and started haranguing people on the street with these questions, how many of those people would have a name for their accountant, dentist, and hair stylist? Probably most of them, right? And many of them could probably also name their doctor, plumber, electrician, architect, and all sorts of other service professionals. But how many of them would also name YOU as their real estate agent?

Honestly, how many of them would name *anyone* as their real estate agent?

I'll tell you what would happen, because I've actually done this.

Most people have an accountant.

Almost all of them have a dentist.

All the women have a hair stylist.

And almost nobody has a real estate agent.

Even if they do have a real estate agent, it's because they're actually in the process of selling or buying a home right at that moment:

they're listed or looking. Or their brother is a real estate agent, something like that.

But if they bought a few years ago? Then they don't think of themselves as "having" a real estate agent. They "had" a real estate agent, but not anymore. Their transaction is over, and relationship has ended.

Why is that? Why do people think of themselves as "having" an accountant, dentist, a hair stylist, or other service professionalism but don't think they "have" a real estate agent?

You might think it's just about the frequency of a transaction. After all, most people (hopefully!) do their taxes every year, and (hopefully!) see their dentist twice a year. And they go to the hair stylist every few months or so, or at least whenever the roots start to show. But most people take years and years between real estate transactions, so that naturally frays whatever connection they might have to their agent.

Okay, maybe that's part of it. But people "have" a lot of service professionals that they only see infrequently. You don't generally need a plumber or an electrician every year. Or an architect. Or a plastic surgeon. But once you've established a relationship with a professional you like and trust, you tend to think of them as "your" provider, even if you don't need your pipes cleared or your face lifted every year. The relationship exists outside the transaction.

In real estate, though, the relationship usually ends when the transaction closes. Part of it is that most agents don't work very hard to keep that relationship going. They generally focus their energies and attention on "leads," endlessly prospecting for people who might be buying or selling within the next six months.

It's understandable, of course: we focus on transactions because that's when we get paid. I get it. But that relentless drive to generate leads sometimes makes us obsess too much about the short-term. A neighbor stops by our open house because she is curious about the layout, and we dismiss her as a "looky-loo." We don't follow up with that call on our listing once we realize they're not looking to move anytime soon. And even though we love those wonderful clients who just bought a house from us, well, they're not going to be moving again anytime soon, are they? So why spend a lot of time on them?

Even worse, because we think transactionally, consumers think transactionally. If we don't pay attention to them, they're not going to pay attention to us. Indeed, rather than see us as service professionals like lawyers or plumbers, they see us strictly as "salespeople"—the "Original Sin." There's nothing inherently wrong with that—after all, sales is a part of what we do. But the problem is that no one "has" a salesperson. People don't feel loyalty to a salesperson. Think of it this way—if you were in the market to buy a car, would you be committed to working with the salesperson who sold you your last car? Not really. No one runs around saying, "you have to buy a car from my guy at Audi!" or "if you're buying clothes, you have to go see Nancy at Macy's – she's the very best!" We simply don't maintain relationships with salespeople the same way they do with service professionals like accountants, dentists, hair stylists, and the rest.

That's why both agents and consumers share a narrow conception of what real estate agents do for clients: help you transact real estate. We think transactionally because that's when we get paid. And people think transactionally because they don't generally maintain ongoing relationships with salespeople.

And by extension, both agents and consumers share a narrow conception of what clients need from agents: assistance in transacting real estate. Essentially, people don't "have" a real estate agent because they think that they only need an agent if they're actively in the market. If they're not buying or selling real estate right now, they don't *need* an agent.

Here's the problem with that way of thinking: it's just not true. People have real estate needs that go well beyond just a real estate transaction. They're not necessarily needs that will generate a sales commission, but they're still real estate needs.

The "Cocktail Party Conversation"

Here's what I mean. Let's say that you're at a cocktail party, or a kid's soccer game, or at a networking event, or hanging out after church or temple or mosque or Satanic Temple, or whatever. The important thing is that you're in a social situation where you meet someone you don't already know. If you can think back to the last time you had a conversation like that, here's what probably happened.

Because you're a sociable person, you probably asked them about themselves and their work. So you asked:

"*So, what do you do?*"

And they said something like:

"*I'm a florist.*"

Or an accountant, or a bartender, or whatever. The point is that they're going to tell you what they do. So, now, you ask them a few more questions about their work, where they live, things like that. If you're a good conversationalist, of course, you know that the best way to build rapport with people is to ask them questions about themselves. So that's what's you did. Then, at some point in the conversation, that florist turned the question back on you. He asked:

"*And what do you do?*"

And you said:

"*I'm in real estate.*"

Okay, stop! Seriously, I want you to think about the last time you had a conversation like that, where you told someone you didn't know that you were in real estate. What's the next question out of their mouths? Do you remember it? It was almost certainly this one:

"*How's the market?*"

You get asked that all the time, don't you? If you introduce yourself to someone, and tell them you're in real estate, they ask you how the market is. Not once in a while. Not sometimes. Not most times. Almost all the time.

Indeed, because I'm both a lawyer and a real estate broker, I have a couple of different ways that I can answer the "what do you do?" question. I've found that if I don't really want to talk to that person, I just tell them I'm a lawyer. That usually ends things. No one wants to talk to a lawyer.

But if I want to get into a conversation, I tell them I'm a real estate broker. Because I know the next thing out of their mouth will be:

"*How's the market?*"

That's a really important question, because it tells us a few things about consumers. For one thing, they're curious about what's going on in the real estate market. They want to know if it's up or down, hot or cold, busy or slow. And that makes sense, because everyone is in the real estate market. They all live somewhere. If they live with their parents, they want to know what's happening with rentals. If they rent, they probably have hopes of someday buying. If they own, they want to know how their investment is doing—and maybe, just maybe, they're thinking of upsizing or downsizing.

The real estate market is unique in that way: not everyone owns stocks, not everyone owns bonds, but everyone has to live somewhere. That's why they're always asking "how's the market?"

That's what we call the "Cocktail Party Conversation" question— you tell someone what you do, and they ask, "How's the market?" It's a really important conversation, because it tells us that people have at least one specific need that goes well beyond the real estate transaction – the need to know how the market is doing.

But the "Cocktail Party Conversation" tells us something even more important: this need isn't being met. These people want to know what's going on in the market, and no one is telling them.

Why? Because they don't "have" an agent. They don't have someone they can turn to when they have real estate questions, something they can rely on, someone they can trust.

And they need one! It's not just about keeping track of the real estate market. Think of all the "non-transactional" real estate questions that consumers have every day. They pass a "for sale" sign on their block, they want to know what it's selling for. They see it come down, they want to know what it sold for. They have questions about their taxes and their mortgage. They need recommendations for a plumber or an electrician or some other professional. They want to know how much their home is worth, maybe for a tax grievance or an insurance valuation. And at any given time, they're thinking of adding another bedroom, or finishing their basement, or putting in a pool, or doing any number of home improvement projects that might impact their property value. Shouldn't they talk to a real estate agent before they spend $50,000 on a new kitchen, just to get an idea of whether they're making a good long-term investment?

And yet, these people rarely call an agent for help. Why? Oddly enough, it's usually because they're too nice. They don't want to bother the agent with questions that don't involve buying or selling. They realize that we only get paid on a transaction, and they're reluctant to "take advantage" of us by asking for free advice. They think of agents as salespeople who help them through a transaction, not as resources for information on all things real estate.

We can't blame them, because that's how we think of ourselves. Consumers are simply following our lead. We think transactionally, so they think transactionally. We pay attention to them only when they're buying or selling, so they pay attention to us only when they're buying or selling.

But isn't it a little convenient that we've chosen to define consumer real estate needs as limited to the need to buy or sell a home? Yes, that's the only time they're willing to pay us, but it's not the only time they need us.

Here's the bottom line: everyone needs a real estate agent. A great real estate agent. All the time. Even when they're not buying or selling.

And that great real estate agent should be you.